# THE
# NORTHUMBRIAN UPLANDS

Looking down the Coquet Valley, near Alwinton, with the Harbottle Hills on the right and the Simonside Hills ahead

# THE
# NORTHUMBRIAN
# UPLANDS

## Geoffrey N. Wright

**David & Charles**
Newton Abbot   London   North Pomfret (Vt)

**British Library Cataloguing in Publication Data**

Wright, Geoffrey N. (Geoffrey Norman), *1925-*
 The Northumbrian uplands.————(David
 & Charles Britain series).
 1. Northumberland. National parks :
 Northumberland National Park – Visitors'
 guides.
 I. Title
 914.28'8

 ISBN 0–7153–9042–2

Thomas Bewick's illustrations by courtesy of the Thomas Bewick
Birthplace Trust, Cherryburn, Stocksfield, Northumberland
Text and illustrations © Geoffrey Wright 1989

Phototypeset by ABM Typographics, Hull
and printed in Great Britain
by Butler & Tanner Limited, Frome and London
for David & Charles Publishers plc
Brunel House Newton Abbot Devon

Distributed in the United States by
David & Charles Inc
North Pomfret Vermont 05053 USA

# CONTENTS

# INTRODUCTION

What the Romans thought of their road from Eboracum to Trimontium – York and Melrose today – is not recorded. For me and thousands of travellers, its northern section, adopted for part of the way by the A68, is a favourite route to Scotland. Once across the River Tyne near Corbridge, and the subsequent climb to Portgate roundabout where the road crosses the line of the Roman Wall, it surges and swoops northwards across the repeated rhythm of the rocks, now grassed over into a crumpled counterpane of spacious landscapes. The road passes shadowy ghosts of villages and their furrowed former fields, lonely churches, huge farmsteads behind their shelter-belts of tall trees, with an occasional hint of a vanished industry. After being joined by the A696 coming up from Newcastle by Otterburn, the road urges you northwards past the military ranges in Redesdale, through the conifer plantations of the Border Forest Park, and beyond Catcleugh Reservoir it starts the long climb to Carter Bar and the Scottish border.

At the top of the hill beyond the River Rede at West Woodburn a re-erected Roman milestone stands sentinel beyond a wall on the left, and the roadside symbol of a curlew indicates that you have entered the Northumberland National Park. For the next five miles the A68 forms part of the eastern boundary of the National Park, and does so again from Byrness to the border, conveniently bisecting the 398 square miles of wild or relatively wild countryside designated our ninth national park in 1956, the most northerly one, the least populated and least visited.

The great historian G. M. Trevelyan, born and brought up at Wallington, now a National Trust property, knew and loved his native

Northumbrian hills largely through years of mainly solitary walking among them. Nobody has better expressed or evoked their character:

> In Northumberland alone, both heaven and earth are seen; we walk all day on long ridges, high enough to give far views of moor and valley, and the sense of solitude far below . . . It is the land of far horizons, where the piled or drifted shapes of gathered vapour are for ever moving along the furthest ridge of hills, like the procession of long primeval ages that is written in tribal mounds and Roman camps and Border towers, on the breast of Northumberland.
>
> Up above here on the moor, the silent sheep browse all day long, filling the mind with thoughts of peace and safety; they seem diligent to compensate themselves for a thousand years of raids and interrupted pasture . . . Northumberland throws over us, not a melancholy, but a meditative spell.

The National Park extends for forty miles from the Roman Wall to the Scottish border embracing great diversity of landscapes forming five distinct groups. Along the Park's southern edge the Roman Wall area is a stretch of country whose historic background makes it unique in Europe. The view northwards from the frowning crags along which the Wall strides leads the eye to the North Tyne valley, and beyond it, in imagination, to the broader uplands embracing the River Rede. North-eastwards again it leads to the fourth region of Park landscape, that of Coquetdale and the curving arc of the Simonside Hills. Stand on their crags and let the eye rove northwards again to an horizon filled with Cheviot Hills, rising in green waves to the great Cheviot ridge where the English and Scots drew their first sketchy boundary, a line fought over for eight centuries.

That boundary followed a natural watershed. The older frontier of the Roman Wall took advantage of a natural geological feature, the Whin Sill outcrop. When the National Park was designated its limits were defined by bureaucrats. Apart from in the north-west where it follows the Scottish border, its course suggests administrative convenience rather than the logic of landscape. Thus, it includes a large block of land under military ownership but excludes good moorland landscapes east of the A696. It includes part of Wark Forest, presumably to link the northern and central sections to the Roman Wall area, but excludes that part of Northumberland extending southwards from the South Tyne, which embraces a fine area of North Pennine country forming the watersheds and valleys of the South Tyne, the East and West Allen, and part of the Derwent, all part of the recently-designated North Pennines Area of Outstanding Natural Beauty, a somewhat tardy recognition of its

*Whittingham Vale and the Cheviot Hills from above Thropton, near Rothbury*

*The South Tyne, by Featherstone Park*

landscape quality. This book is concerned with the Northumbrian Uplands, mainly the National Park but including those areas bordering it already mentioned, together with the rest of the North Tyne valley and Redesdale south-east of the Park boundary roughly as far as the line of the old Corn Road, represented by the A6079 and B6342. Additionally, the English part of the Border Forest Park, designated at the same time as the National Park, and adjoining it on the west, is included.

Except in the forest plantations which were just appearing on the landscape when he wrote sixty years ago, Trevelyan's description is still relevant. Most of the area is upland country, usually sombre in colour, a broad wash of greens and various shades of brown. In Cheviot valleys and Coquetdale, gorse blazes into golden glory as though to celebrate the late-arriving spring. By June ash and birch, beech and oak are greening the hedgerows, shelter-belts and copses, and the mantle of flowers in valley meadows and by riversides is at its brightest. Heather moorland matures into purple splendour in late August, and September sees the first turning of the leaves. Among these northern hills winters are long, often with severe cold spells, and the A68 is one of the first roads to be blocked by snow, usually at Carter Bar. An unfriendly land and a hostile climate offer a harsh welcome to the late-April lambs.

*(pp10-11) East Allendale, below Allenheads, looking north*

If I were to show a visitor the National Park at its best I should take him to upper Coquetdale in October, when autumn burnishes the brackeny lower slopes of the hills, and the birches glow in a harmony of silver and gold. Even the roadside view is richly satisfying, but a riverside stroll or a walk in Holystone woods bring richer rewards. Best of all would be a sunny second Saturday in October when the Annual Border Shepherds' Show at Alwinton provides the setting, the warmth, the music and the human dimension of the perfect, intimate country show.

For me and many others walking is the best way physically to experience landscape, to become absorbed into it, and feel its changes of mood. Senses perceive its subtleties of colour, of light and shade and the changing shapes of clouds, sounds of wind and water and the call of birds, scents of flowers, fungus, and the earth after freshening rain. Booted feet appreciate the difference between sandstone tracks on Simonside, squelching peat on Cheviot, crisp smooth turf on lower slopes and by the Wall. Cool, clean water of brown burns is a satisfying benison for tired feet after a long tramp on the high hills.

*The northern face of the Cheviot Hills, from the Scottish side of the Border, near Town Yetholm*

The Planning Committee of the National Park is a separate committee of the Northumberland County Council and includes members appointed directly by the Secretary of State for the Environment after consultation with the Countryside Commission. Its objectives can conveniently be summarised as:

1  To preserve and enhance the natural beauty of the area.
2  To promote its enjoyment by the public.
3  To have due regard to the needs of agriculture and forestry and to the social and economic interests of the area.

Generally, conservation of landscape character, natural and man-made, and of wildlife, takes priority over recreation. Promotion of public enjoyment is interpreted as providing opportunity without positively encouraging indiscriminate recreational expansion. Most visitors come by car and enjoy relatively passive sightseeing and touring. Public transport facilities are meagre to say the least. Daily buses serve Wooler, via the A696, Redesdale via the A68, the North Tyne and South Tyne valleys. Irregular services operate between Hexham and Redesdale, and beyond Wooler, while the Post Bus is a facility enjoyed by Coquetdale people from Thropton to Alwinton. The only useful railway is that of the Newcastle-Carlisle line, operated by diesel railcar units.

An increasing number of visitors come to enjoy walking, particularly on the moors and hills, and it could be reasonably claimed that the central section of the Roman Wall is the most popular historic walk in England. Cycling is popular without ever being likely to become dominant, and for water-sports enthusiasts Kielder Water in the Border Forest Park caters for almost all types of enjoyment. Boat-launching facilities, canoeing, dinghy-sailing, surf-boarding and boat-hire operate from the main base of Leaplish, but power-boating is not permitted at the moment. Worm and fly-fishing are available from bank or boat. Anglers will enjoy good fishing on the Coquet above Rothbury, the North Tyne above Bellingham and the lower part of the Rede.

Only about 2,000 people live within the National Park, but a number of settlements are located on or near its margins, with Hexham (10,000) by far the largest. Haltwhistle (3,500), Corbridge (2,500), Haydon Bridge (2,000), Rothbury (1,800), Wooler (1,800), Bellingham (800) and Allendale Town (800) are the others that can be considered more than villages. However, it has been calculated that about four million people live within two hours driving time of the Park boundaries, a relatively low figure compared with corresponding figures for most of the other National Parks.

The historic appeal of the Roman Wall area makes it a honeypot attraction, helped undoubtedly by its ease of access from the motorways A1(M) and M6 at its eastern and western ends, with the improved trunk

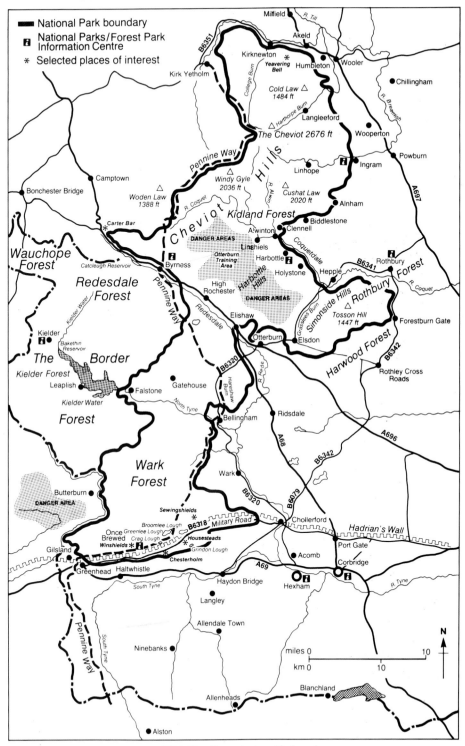

**The Northumbrian Uplands**

*Housesteads Fort, on Hadrian's Wall, showing part of the headquarters building with barrack blocks beyond*

road, A69, along the Tyne valley linking them. Problems facing earlier travellers must have been unbelievably daunting. Leland, in the 1540s, touched the eastern and southern fringes of the National Park area. Fifty years later Camden visited and wrote the first important account of the Roman Wall, and at the end of the seventeenth century Celia Fiennes, riding side-saddle through England, also visited the 'Picts' Wall', stayed at Haltwhistle in a poor cottage, and continued her journey through Haydon Bridge to Hexham, Corbridge and Newcastle. By the last quarter of the eighteenth century, following Arthur Young's travels, the 'Agricultural Tour' was replacing the 'Grand Tour'.

For the topographers and artists, and even the 'curious' traveller, the castles of the east and the houses of large landowners were the attractions. The remote beauties of the uplands were largely ignored. Girtin painted a view of the Tyne at Hexham in 1800 and Samuel Buck painted Brinkburn Priory in 1728, also recorded in characteristically dramatic form a century later by Turner.

With so much of Roman interest the antiquarians were more adventurous. Even their enthusiasm could hardly match that of a seventy-eight-year old Birmingham shopkeeper who, in 1801, set off from his home to walk to the Wall, at Solway, to walk it to Wallsend and back again, before walking home to Birmingham. William Hutton's mammoth 600-mile walk took only thirty-five days, and he was quite dottily overjoyed by the experience. Present-day visitors probably reckon that half a day at Housesteads and nearby is sufficient.

National Parks are neither national nor are they parks. Most land within their arbitrary boundaries is privately owned, with no automatic right of access. Most is farmed, and different farmers and landowners manage it in different ways. But it is those same people, and their forbears over successive generations, who have shaped and tended the landscapes we see and appreciate. It is they today who have to live their lives and face the problems of visitor pressures. Hill-farming is a chancy business, and in the increasing worries about its long-term viability it could well be that in the end hill-farmers may become glorified park-keepers, paid to keep things going for the benefit of visitors.

In the Northumberland National Park, alternative land uses are starkly illustrated. About one-fifth is owned by the Forestry Commission, and rather more than a fifth by the Ministry of Defence, thus producing the paradox that, in an area where most land is privately owned, those areas which, in effect, the taxpayer has paid for are those to which access is most strictly limited. The Forestry Commission is recognising to an increasing degree the recreational needs of visitors, and has waymarked many miles of walks and bridleways through the forests, and created a number of scenic laybys, carparks and picnic sites. But public enjoyment is always, one feels, on the Commission's terms. There is only a controlled freedom.

The Otterburn ranges in Redesdale are closed to the public on at least 300 days each year. They *are* open on some Bank Holidays, over Christmas, and from 15 April–15 May when lambing occurs. I have seen very little public use of the Army roads or lonelier tracks during those open times, and to be quite honest, the landscapes they cover are of little scenic interest compared to those available elsewhere in the Park. It would, though, be of the greatest use to the public if two of the roads linking Coquetdale with Redesdale (Chew Green to Cottonshopefoot and Holystone to Rochester) were open much more often, enabling visitors to link these valleys in circular tours over some of the wildest Park scenery.

I first walked along the exciting middle section of the Roman Wall in 1943 while staying with a group of students at Once Brewed Youth Hostel. Since then I have visited it, and the rest of the Northumbrian Uplands, repeatedly, and always with great joy. Their elemental landscapes, spacious solitudes, windy hills and quick brown rivers never fail to appeal; but perhaps it is the rich historical humus which is the secret ingredient, the essence of Northumbrian magic. Dwellers in remote Iron Age forts, Roman legions, Pictish tribes, Celtic missionary saints, border reivers, smugglers, drovers and generations of farmers have travelled the same tracks, seen similar views beneath cool northern skies. The past is always present in what was, in centuries past, any man's kingdom.

*Part of the massive rampart wall of the Iron Age hill fort at Yeavering Bell, near Wooler. In the distance are The Cheviot (right) and Hedgehope (left)*

# 1

# MAKING OF THE LANDSCAPE

Rocks are the basis of land-forms and scenery, and the geological history of the Northumberland Uplands is, in general terms, fairly clearly displayed if not always simple to explain. It needs to be realised at the outset, however, that the east-west corridor formed by the valley of the River Tyne, the 'Tyne Gap' of geography textbooks, is not only a prominent and important physical feature but also represents a real geographical divide. A short journey down the valleys of the South Tyne or the Allendales presents a vastly different picture from the scene enjoyed from the Military Road, in its course parallel to the Roman Wall. Contrasting still more is the swift arrowing northwards of the A68 route to Scotland via Carter Bar as it rolls and rides the rhythmic crests of the rocks, always with open views to east and west. If its landscapes show Northumberland at its most spacious, the road from Rothbury up Coquetdale, narrowing at Alwinton, insinuates itself, secretive and snakelike, through narrow passes between steep-sided green hills until, at Makendon within a mile of the Border, it ends in loneliness and a military presence.

An appraisal of the geological factors which have fashioned these varied landscapes best starts with the oldest, which are also the highest, in the far north, and the story spans almost 400 million years. Indeed, almost all the rocks which make up the Northumbrian landscape are much older than the European Alps, yet are still younger than the hills of

Lakeland to the west. Additionally, for almost half the time that has elapsed since the rocks were formed the Northumbrian uplands have been a land-surface subjected to millions of years of weathering which has worn them down close to their original roots. The whole platform of ancient rocks has been faulted, folded, compressed, uplifted, subjected to earthquake and volcanoes, and changed by the Ice Age whose glacial agents of erosion and deposition have produced some of the most significant features of the landscape.

The rocks of the Cheviot Hills are entirely igneous, derived as molten material from inside the earth probably about 380 million years ago, in the Lower Old Red Sandstone or Devonian Period of geological time. Originating as a series of violent volcanic eruptions centred probably on a crater west of the present Cheviot summit, huge masses of rock debris varying in size from small pellets to pieces bigger than footballs (called pyroclasts), were thrown into the air to fall as a thick deposit of lava called andesite. Above Coquethead, the hill of Thirlmoor, 1,833ft (558m) is largely formed of this material, deposited many miles from its volcanic source. Nearby, it can also be seen in the banks of the Coquet between Fulhope and Makendon, while there are good exposures in the Breamish valley, by the road to Linhope.

Weathering has altered these andesite lavas to pink, purple or grey colours, usually speckled, and less frequently in their unweathered condition having a black, more glassy surface veined with red jasper. Examples of this form occur at Kilham Hill, 885312, and Longknowe, 875302. Upon these deposits of andesite successive flows of lava, extruded probably from a number of craters, gradually solidified into thousands of feet of thickness which today forms the main bulk of the Cheviot Hills, on both sides of the Border line.

Subsequent surges of subterranean activity brought more masses of magma to the surface, melting as it did so the adjoining rocks and solidified lavas which it encountered. Eventually it subsided within the main body of Cheviot lavas, creating a great core of granite which now forms the highest land in the Cheviots. Originally this could have reached a height of 15,000 to 20,000ft, now reduced to a mere 2,673ft (815m). Some of the volcanic magma never reached the surfaces but slowly cooled at great depths.

Millions of years of erosion have now brought some of these plutonic rocks to the surface; the pink Cheviot granites around Hedgehope, at the head of Langleeford, and forming the domed plateau of Cheviot itself, once lay at the heart of an ancient volcano. The outcrop of unusually bright pink granite at the Harden quarry near Biddlestone is probably the most vivid exposure of this rock.

Rocks whose structure is changed by heat and pressure are known as metamorphic. Andesite lavas thus affected by the later intrusion of

Cheviot granite were hardened, and made more weather-resistant, so that they are now represented by the occasional tor-like outcrops seen above the Harthope valley. Housey Crags, Long Crags and Middleton Crags, all east of Langleeford, are good examples, and the public right-of-way that climbs southwards from Langlee allows a closer view of these features. On the west side of Cheviot, the Schil, Henhole and Braydon Crag on West Hill, above the College valley, all represent exposures of this metamorphic aureole which surrounds the Cheviot, but there are few exposures of the granite itself since most of it is covered by thick peat, as walkers on the Cheviot plateau know only too well. However, to the north of the Breamish valley, Great and Little Standrop are tors of granite, while Cunyan Crags, 978182 on the eastern spur of Dunmoor Hill, add a slightly Dartmoorian element to the smooth green slopes. Linhope Spout, 959171, an attractive and well-known waterfall on the Linhope Burn at the head of the Breamish valley, shows one of the best exposures of the grey Cheviot granite.

Thus, the highest and wildest parts of the Cheviots represent its granite core, where peat is abundant and heather dominates. The surrounding andesite aureole, at an average height of 1,500ft (457m), and with its more crumbly nature, is identified by its deeply eroded valleys and its lighter-coloured vegetation, supporting grass and bracken, but generally too lime-rich for heather.

When the Cheviots were formed, and the process of weathering started its relentless attack, the volcanoes and their metamorphic aureole were surrounded by water. Erosion gradually brought down to the shore-line enormous quantities of boulders and pebbles, spreading them out, fan-like in the shallows, where they consolidated into conglomerates, recognised today as the high cliffs in the gorge of Roddam Dene, 025206, six miles south of Wooler. Finer deposits of sand and mud were slowly laid down on the sea-bed above the conglomerates, forming alternating layers of sandstones and shales. Under the accumulated weight of these deposits the sea-bed subsided, and there were periods of time in which various forms of marine life flourished in the clear seas. These lime-bearing organisms eventually created the limestones which were added to the existing strata, whose resulting sequence of sandstones, shales, and limestones forms the earliest rocks of the Carboniferous system in Northumberland, where because of the clayey nature of the limestone strata, the succession is known as the Cementstones. In Coquetdale above Alwinton the steep cliffs of Barrow Scar, 903062, above the river's south bank are the best exposure in the area of these sedimentary rocks which originated in shallow seas about 340 million years ago. Glebe

*Upper Coquetdale, from the Pass Peth, an historic border track*

Quarry, *052007*, south of Rothbury reveals an unusually thick bed of limestone from the Cementstones series.

The Cementstones form a girdle round the northern, eastern and southern margins of the Cheviots, and in landscape terms are responsible for the low hills extending from Whittingham Vale south-westwards to Coquetdale near Hepple, but were sufficiently soft to allow the River Aln to cut a course eastwards through them to Alnwick and the sea. The Cementstones are continuous south-westwards, forming the low, featureless country in Redesdale and the upper part of the North Tyne valley.

Overlying the Cementstones and therefore younger than them is a thick succession of Fell Sandstones laid down originally as the vast delta of a river which must have drained an enormous land mass then lying across the north Atlantic. Again, alternate subsidence and deposition of sandy sediments to thicknesses of 500 to 1,000ft (152 to 305m) in different parts of the region have yielded rocks which today form some of the most characteristic features of the landscape of central Northumberland. Indeed, more than any other rock it seems to me to symbolise the county, and is unique to it. Beautiful in texture and colour, durable but difficult to work, it has created not only fine landscapes, but also notable buildings. Northumberland is the only English county in which these Lower Carboniferous Sandstones have been extensively used for building, obtained from a number of different quarries, with those near Fourstones, west of Hexham, among the most famous. Stone from there was chosen by John Dobson, 1846–50, for his great Newcastle Central Station. Seventeen centuries earlier the Romans used this Fell Sandstone for the facing blocks of Hadrian's Wall.

Much of the beauty comes from the traceried patterns of its weathering along joint lines and the original bedding planes in the sands laid down so long ago. Climbers like its cracks and chimneys, walkers are happy merely to appreciate the dramatic nature of its outcrops, especially on the Simonside and Harbottle Hills south of the Coquet. Past convulsions of the earth have heaved, forced, folded and faulted this solid sandstone to create two wide, broken arcs of high ground that swing across the middle of the county, almost from Berwick to the Cumbrian border in an elongated S shape. The northern half of the Fell Sandstone outcrop is a constant escarpment, with steep, strong crags always facing inwards to Cheviot, and the gentle dip-slope running away to the east and south. Such asymmetrical ridges are called cuestas and central Northumberland is cuesta country *par excellence.* The Fell Sandstones break down into an acid soil, rich in silica, and, like granite, support the growth of heather.

*The Breamish Valley, above Ingram*

*Langlee Crags, looking north-west to Housey Crag (centre) and The Cheviot beyond*

Walk on any of the tempting tracks on the Simonside Hills, on the moors north of Rothbury, or on the Harbottle Hills, and you are immediately aware of the coarse sandy texture of the soil, and the vegetation it supports. Similarly, the view southwards from Coquetdale, between Rothbury and Hepple, Hareshaw and Holystone, shows the dark, frowning crags of the north scarp face.

To the west the Fell Sandstones form most of the high land south of the Border between Carter Fell and the Bewcastle Fells of Cumbria. Subsequent faulting has had the effect of chopping up this stretch of country, now largely afforested, into a series of blocks, resulting in the high ridges of Deadwater Fell, Mid Fell, Peel Fell, and Oh Me Edge while the occasional outcrops from Wylies Crags to Christianbury Crags are reminders of the resistant nature of this rock. The Forest Drive between Kielder and Byrness gives a good series of views of this Fell Sandstone country between the North Tyne and Redesdale.

Overlying, and hence younger than, the Fell Sandstones, is the Scremerston Series, 3,800ft (1,170m) of limestones, sandy-limestones and sandstones, interbedded with shales and coal-seams. Except for a large enclave in Redesdale between Elsdon and Corsenside, the Scremerston Series forms a band about a dozen miles wide running south-westwards across the area, most of it moorland country now under forest. However, much of it, represented on the surface by sandstones, still presents a, rugged and inhospitable appearance, especially on the Ottercops, 1,022ft (312m), the Wannies, 1,000ft (305m) and Corsenside Common, 1,198ft (365m). The Rede and the North Tyne have cut through to a series of more shaley strata, which, being more fertile, have resulted in better land use, but it is the coal seams, some of the earliest formed in Britain, which have been most exploited, and it is significant that it is the Scremerston Coals which have given the name to the whole series of strata. Details of coal-mining are given in a later chapter.

Just as these strata succeeded the older Fell Sandstones to the north, so are they succeeded by Carboniferous Limestones to the south, reaching to and beyond the valley of the Tyne. Within them more sandstones occur, producing small areas of moorland and occasionally outcropping as low crags, miniature versions of the Simonside escarpment. Rothley Crags, north of Scots Gap, and Shaftoe Crags east of Kirkharle, are typical examples, while well-farmed sweet pastures invariably indicate the presence of limestone. A journey along the A68 takes you across the grain of the rocks, the gentle gradients as you travel north from the Portgate, above Corbridge, taking you up the almost insignificant dip-slope, with the occasional sharp descents representing north-facing escarpments of sandstone, although the rock itself is usually hidden beneath glacial deposits of thick boulder-clay.

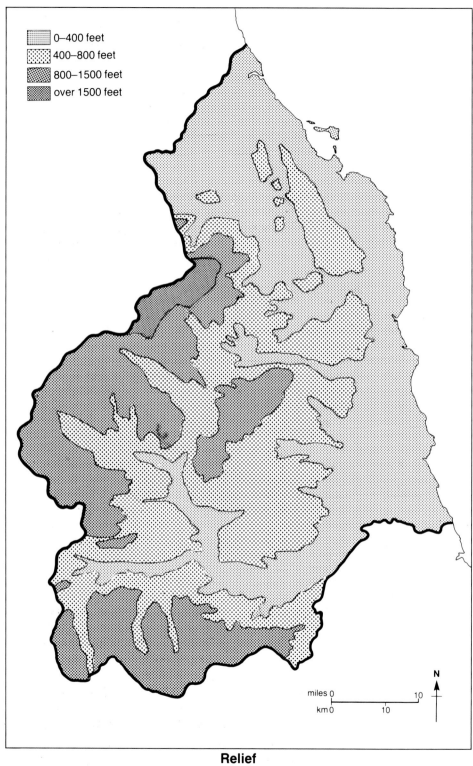

0–400 feet
400–800 feet
800–1500 feet
over 1500 feet

miles 0    10
km 0    10

N

**Relief**

Volcanic activity produced the highest ground at the northern edge of the National Park. Near the Park's southern boundary, volcanic activity of a later date, though not producing surface eruptions here, created a particularly impressive landscape feature occurring only in northern England.

The Whin Sill seems to have been a lava flow originating at different times, far to the west, but introducing itself as a molten sheet between rocks in the Carboniferous strata. It is an igneous rock which solidified underground, the resultant slow cooling producing a coarse-textured, crystalline dolerite, mainly dark blue-grey in colour on a fresh, unweathered specimen, but turning buff or grey on exposure to the air. Varying in thickness, but averaging just under 100ft (30m), it has formed a series of sills across northern England, and, being far more resistant to erosion than the sandstones and shales where it occurs, it has created numerous escarpments, none so dramatic as that on which the Romans built their Wall, especially in its central section west of Sewingshields, with the rugged crags above Crag Lough one of the most memorable highlights of landscape within the National Park. The partial columnar jointing of these near-vertical crags provides rock-climbers with many challenging routes.

Looking northwards from the Whin Sill outcrop the view reveals succeeding parallel ridges of sandstone, petrified waves in a landscape, conifer-blanketed beyond. Between some of the ridges, ice action has gouged out deep basins, some once filled with lakes that have now dried out, leaving great deposits of peat. In others, the lakes survive, with Broomlee, Greenlee and Crag Loughs remaining as attractive stretches of open water.

Southwards from the Wall the land dips to the South Tyne valley, a fault-line corridor, river-worn, ice-eroded and thickly covered with glacial drift. The valley marks the northern limit of the Pennines, and the land to its south has a distinctive unity which creates a sharp contrast to the rest of the Northumbrian uplands. Geologists call it the 'Alston Block', and it is based on Cross Fell, 2,930ft (893m), highest of the Pennine peaks.

Three great northern rivers, Tees, Wear and South Tyne, are born within a few miles of one another on Cross Fell's massive bulk. Two flow generally eastwards but the Tyne takes a northwards course. Until the Ice Age it turned westwards near Haltwhistle and flowed to the Solway, but huge amounts of glacial drift subsequently forced it into its present valley, swinging eastwards near Featherstone. Minor spurs extending north-eastwards from Cross Fell have created watersheds for the other rivers draining away in that direction, West and East Allen, Devil's Water and the Derwent, all with much shorter valleys than that of the Tyne. Between them are the gritstone moors of north Pennine country, highest

in the west – Grey Nag, above Whitley Common in the far south-west of Northumberland, 2,152ft (656m) high, is not a peak but merely the highest point on an elevated plateau several square miles in area.

From Grey Nag the land dips gently to the north and east, still wild moorland country, dark and dour, a sea of heather moors and mosses. Farther east, between the Allendales, and between East Allendale, the Devil's Water and the Derwent, the gritstone moors are drier, support more heather, and provide some of the best grouse-shooting in England. Within their limestone strata, rich veins of lead-ore were intruded in Carboniferous times – possibly contemporary with the Whin Sill – giving an economic importance to the Allendales, in particular in the eighteenth and nineteenth centuries. Some of the sandstones yielded good building and roofing materials, so that accidents of geology have created in the Northumbrian uplands south of the Tyne, not only landscapes and scenery different from those to the north, but valleys where stone walls enclose pastures, farmsteads are more numerous, and villages show a more nucleated structure.

Although rocks are the skeletal foundation of landscape and scenery, the landforms seen today owe a great deal to the effects of the Ice Ages, which lasted about one million years and ended about 12000 BC. In Britain, the vast northern ice-sheet of Arctic origins and character extended as far south as the Thames valley and the coast of South Wales. In the Pennines it filled all the valleys and covered the uplands to about 2,100ft (650m), and on the Cheviots it reached about 1,750ft (533m). Thus, at the greatest extent of glaciation only the highest parts of the region stood out above the thick apron of ice, which, although it thinned towards the east, was still several hundred feet thick.

Huge glaciers moved slowly across the land, southwards from Scotland, where the Cheviots deflected them into smaller ice-streams. Scandinavian ice choked the North Sea basin, forcing south-flowing Scottish ice down the eastern side of Northumberland. Ice moving northwards down the Vale of Eden encountered more Scottish ice, and some of it was deflected eastwards beyond Brampton and along the Tyne gap. Moving ice scoured the landscape, smoothed hillsides and removed surface soil and boulders. This eroded material was carried by the glaciers, and when the ice eventually and slowly melted it was deposited as boulder clay, thinly in the uplands but much more thickly in valleys as transverse and lateral moraines, along valley floors, and over the lower land to the east. In the Tyne gap west of Haltwhistle this glacial drift is marked by drumlins, small oval-shaped hills of boulder clay and pebbles deposited and shaped along the grain of glacier-flow. Some rise to between 50 and

*Climbers above Crag Lough*

100ft (15 and 30m) above the intervening hollows, sufficient sometimes to be indicated by contours on the map, but far more easily identified in the field.

Accumulated glacial drift between Haltwhistle and Gilsland caused other changes, including alteration in river-flow. Before glaciation the upper Irthing followed a course which took it south-eastwards to the Tyne near Haltwhistle. Drift deposition then blocked its path, diverting its drainage southwards towards Gilsland, where the Irthing Gorge, on the National Park boundary, 630680, is a SSSI. At Gilsland, the Irthing swings westwards to join the Eden near Carlisle.

Although the tops of the Cheviots were not covered by Scottish ice it seems probable that conditions were such that they developed a small ice-cap of their own. Some features near the summit of Cheviot suggest ice moulding. The Henhole, 886202, and the Bizzle, 898222, are very similar to mountain corries, eroded by local glaciers after the main ice-sheet had melted. The steep cliffs of the Bizzle have screes below, a hollowed-out floor, and a marked 'step' in the valley profile with moraines beneath, while the Lambden Burn drains northwards in a valley almost certainly glacier-scooped.

This scouring-out of basins above soft strata such as shales has given Northumberland its 'little lakeland' landscape to the north of the Whin Sill. Here, the cuesta escarpment lay across the glacier-flow, impeding but not stopping the southwards movement of the ice, which gouged out the hollows now occupied by Broomlee, Greenlee and Crag Loughs, none of which is more than ten feet deep. The rocks beneath the Fell Sandstone cuesta were more resistant to such glacial erosion, and the effect of the ice on that escarpment was to erode it, soften it, and lower it.

It is in the Cheviot country that the Ice Ages have had the most prominent effects on the landscape. The smooth, rounded shape of the hills themselves is largely the result of ice-moulding, and while the valleys all existed before them, glaciation and the subsequent torrents of meltwater deepened them, and in a number of cases, widened valley floors. A short climatic improvement which followed the end of the Ice Ages was in turn succeeded by a brief return of very cold conditions when periglacial, or ice-affected, processes continued their erosive attack on surface features. One of these was solifluction, the slow downward movement on hillsides of debris and saturated soil, with its subsequent deposition on valley floors. More meltwaters have cut channels in this material, so that in many valleys streams have been braided, splitting and rejoining repeatedly along their course. Where this process has continued over long periods of time, prominent terraces are formed, subsequently stabilising and supporting vegetation.

*Henhole at the head of the College Valley*

Harthope valley above Langlee shows many of these features. The road follows a river terrace on the north side of the valley to Langleeford, giving good views of the meandering course of the stream, and, on the opposite side, the track climbing between Housey Crags and Langlee Crags starts alongside a prominent meltwater channel called the Shank. The flat valley floor itself emphasises the smoothing action of the glacier that filled it, while the narrow V-shape of the small Hawsen Burn, entering it from the north, is largely unchanged by ice action and owes its form entirely to water erosion.

Terraces are also prominent in the College valley at Hethpool, 895284, where streams show the typical braiding of a glaciated valley. Although the straight course of the valley is the result of faulting, a lateral moraine near Hethpool towards the end of the Ice Ages probably blocked the previous exit taken by the water which eventually found a new outlet to the south and east of The Bell, 901288, where the College Burn carved a gorge through the andesites.

Meltwater channels are landscape features readily identified in the Cheviot Hills. Most are now dry but have a number of points in common, being invariably V-shaped, steep-sided, originating as mature valleys but ending abruptly. They frequently cut across spurs of land, but having carried their torrents at the end of the glaciation and melting period, when normal drainage returned, these channels were left high and dry. Their orientation in the north indicates that water originally from above the College Burn followed a high-level course south of Yeavering Bell and White Law, keeping south of Harehope Hill and Humbleton Hill, and to the west of Wooler. Indeed, Monday Cleugh above Humbleton is both dramatic and historic, being a fine meltwater channel and in more recent times the scene of one of the many battles between the Percys and the Douglases.

Glendale was the site of a deep lake gouged out by ice action in what is now Milfield Plain, an extraordinary area north of Wooler, white on the map with no contours for miles. It must have been one of the biggest hollows in the country, for borings have proved a thickness of 180ft (55m) of fine clay. Its outlet to the south was Shawdon Dene between Glanton and Powburn, now the route of the A697 and the former railway adjoining. The post-glacial drainage took a different route, along the present Vale of Till, meandering northwards past Crookham and Etal to the Tweed. The Powburn channel, like most of the meltwater channels, was probably created by huge torrents flowing under great pressure through tunnels beneath the ice sheet.

Glacial till – the finer material deposited by meltwater, or even by the ice itself when it had lost its mixed constituents – provides excellent farming land, and, in valleys and along the eastern margins of the hills, the edge of land well cultivated marks the limit of such glacial deposits.

The meandering courses of rivers through their valleys, resulting in the deposition of more fine material has resulted in fine, friable soils, sometimes light and sandy, sometimes with more loam, represented by the low-lying landscapes to the west of Hexham and in Glendale. Alluvial deposits, which are frequently also gravelly loams, are invariably called 'haughs' in Northumberland, and while their level nature and good fertility compared with adjoining land make them important agriculturally, their liability to flooding militates against their being suitable settlement sites. Thus, farmsteads and villages keep to the drier ground on the upper edges of the haughs, as in the Coquet valley above Rothbury, as well as along the two Tyne valleys. Around Glendale, Kirknewton, Coupland, Milfield and Doddington further illustrate how early settlers had a sure eye for a site.

Names of certain landscape features also reflect scenic diversity and a recognition of different characteristics. Thus, 'dale' occurs in place-names associated with broad, open valleys of pre-glacial origin, where subsequent glacial erosion and deposition has smoothed their floors. Smaller, but open, tributary valleys are called 'hopes', while post-glacial cuttings by rushing meltwaters are described as 'denes' in Northumberland and Durham. In the hills, especially the Cheviots, the overflow channels of meltwaters and youthful cleft-like gullies on valley sides share the name 'cleughs'.

It has taken almost 400 million years to shape the Northumbrian landscape of today. Although the agents of geological change are constantly at work the effects are so imperceptible that we can scarcely recognise them. A rockfall, a landslip, more river-gravel deposited, or a stream undercutting at a bend – these may be reminders of the relentless process of change, against which man's contribution of less than 10,000 years seems insignificant. But in terms of landscape change they have been enormous, and it is his contribution that must next be considered.

# 2

# FIGURES IN THE LANDSCAPE

In terms of archaeology Man is a latecomer to the Northumbrian scene, and there is no firm evidence for Mesolithic occupation anywhere in the uplands. Although by 3000BC the wooded landscape reached to about 2,000ft (610m), and its wild boar, wild cattle and deer probably attracted small bands of 'hunter-gatherers', their wandering existence has left no traces to satisfy archaeologists. However, by about 2000BC some woodland may have been cleared, yet there is still minimal evidence of permanent settlement, and this is related to Neolithic burials.

On the southern slopes of Dod Hill, *987207*, above Ilderton a long cairn, no more than a pile of stones, 75ft (24m) long and nearly 5ft (1.5m) high probably marks the site of a communal grave. In the heart of the National Park, south of Monkridge in Redesdale, a similar cairn, *911905*, looks forlornly northwards beyond the confluence of the Rede and the Elsdon Burn, as though recognising a fellow object on Bellshiel Law, *812012*, to the west of Dere Street. This has obviously been much disturbed, yet is still an impressive if mute survivor of nearly 4,000 years ago, 350ft (107m) long and 60ft (18m) wide at its broader eastern end. A similar one, hard to find in the forest a mile east of Kielder, is called the Devil's Lapful, *642929*.

Soon after the beginning of the second millenium BC new colonisers, the Beaker-folk from the Rhineland and Low Countries, entered the county on the east coast and gradually penetrated westwards along the river valleys. Their early stone-using economy slowly developed into a metal-based one, but again, evidence of this Bronze Age settlement in

Northumberland comes from their burial mounds. On Garleigh Moor above Rothbury, stone-lined burial cists at Lordenshaw, 061991, are scattered among the heather, while farther up Coquetdale the so-called Five Barrows above Holystone, 953020, are additional evidence for the apparent popularity of this area for early Bronze Age people. Often associated with such burials are the enigmatic 'cup-and-ring' marked stones, and particularly good examples of these are easily seen near the Lordenshaw camp, 055992 and 057992. On Weetwood Moor east of Wooler another group of similarly sculptured stones lie near a stone cairn, 025283, about 218yd (200m) from the Chatton road corner. The significance of cup-and-ring markings is not understood, but they may have had some religious connection. Stone slabs in Bronze Age burial cists have been found with similar markings carved on them. In and around the National Park area they usually occur at various places on the Fell Sandstone arc, and a lesser-known example can be seen at Tod Crag, on Ottercops Moss, 972891, less than a mile from the A696.

A few stone circles within the area probably belong to about the middle of the second millenium (1600–1500BC). The large stone circle at Threestoneburn, 971205, 100 ft (30m) in diameter, may be evidence of ceremonial activity. It should, incidentally, be Thirteen Stone Burn, although only five of the stones are still upright. More accessible though more fragmented is the stone circle, more of a horseshoe, beyond Hethpool in the College valley, 893278. The Goatstones, near Ravensheugh Crags, 831748, south-west of Wark, have in their name and rather bleak setting that aura of mystery so often associated with enigmatic stone circles, as well as those isolated or small groups of standing stones elsewhere in and around the National Park area which may have formed part of larger groupings or alignments. The Mare and Foal, near the Military Road, 726664, north-east of Haltwhistle, may be an example of such a group, while the stones known as the Five Kings (reduced to four) on Woodhouse Beacon in Coquetdale almost invite the creation of suitable legends.

Around 1000BC it appears that the climate became cooler and wetter. It may have been this, together with the gradual influx of new settlers, that brought about changes in types of settlement. More substantial community settlements replaced earlier ones of unenclosed huts, with more attention given to the needs of defence. Closely-packed round timber houses, fifteen to twenty in number, were enclosed within wooden stockades covering about an acre (0.4ha); later, earthen and stone ramparts replaced the stockades, and the late Bronze Age occupants were probably pastoral farmers. Knowledge of these homesteads comes through excavations on later hill-forts which succeeded them, whose ramparts appear frequently to have been built on the same sites as the older defences.

*A cup-and-ring marked stone on Garleigh Moor, below Simonside*

In the cultural lag which affected northern settlement in prehistoric times no sharp line can be drawn between the late Bronze Age and the Iron Age, although it is likely that new waves of immigrants from the continent were infiltrating into existing settlements about the fifth century BC. Iron technology was certainly available then, but there is little evidence to show that it made much impact on these remote areas. However, the newcomers did represent the first large-scale settlement in the National Park area, even if it does seem to be concentrated in the area of the Cheviots and their foothills and valleys. The northern Pennines show little if any evidence of such settlement. It may be, of course, that settlements on lower ground have simply been obliterated by later farming and occupation.

During late Iron Age times, immediately prior to the Roman occupation, a northward movement of Celtic people from lands south of the Tyne introduced the use of iron into Northumberland, and archaeological evidence suggests that they also brought with them the technique for building hill-forts, which are so numerous on the northern Border hills, where there is scarcely a valley spur without its fort, camp, or settlement. On the ground it is usually difficult if not impossible to distinguish between these, but the Ordnance Survey seems to have adopted the distinction that if the earthworks are on a hill summit, or where they suggest the needs of defence, the feature is a hill-fort. The conical shape of so many hills lends itself to simple fort construction, one or more embankments of earth and stones girdling the summits of scores of hills, but each rarely more than an acre (0.4ha) in extent. Their distribution follows the foothills of the central Cheviot massif, from the far north at Pawston Hill, 850319, above the Bowmont, by Yeavering, Harehope, Humbleton, Brough Law and Cochrane Pike above the Breamish, 013146, and south-westwards by Alnham Castlehill, 980110, to the Coquetdale sites at Clennel, 925078, Campville, 948025, and the system on Lordenshaw south of Rothbury. Redesdale and the Tyne valleys have fewer sites, although the near neighbours on Colwellhill, 907938, and Fawden Hill, 897940, between Elsdon and Otterburn indicate that some settlement was established before Agricola pushed his road northwards two miles to the west. At Barcombe, 781668, above Chesterholm, is a rare example of physical juxtaposition of a pre-Roman promontory fort with a Roman military structure, a small signal station.

More hill-forts mark the Fell Sandstone summits east of the Vale of Till, at Dod Law, Chatton, Ross Castle and Old Bewick. Of these, Ross Castle, 081253, above the woods of Chillingham Park, is the most easily accessible and much of it is now National Trust property. Old Bewick, 075216, a few miles south, is even more rewarding, with three visible sets of ditches and stone walls rising to the central enclosure where the ancient huts stood. The ditches are remarkably deep, and the site commands a wide area of landscape, so that one wishes, not for the first time, that the Iron Age Celts who chose and occupied it and others similar could have given us some greater hints of their attitudes, beliefs and skills than these defensive structures merely imply.

Both Ross and Old Bewick are more impressive than many of their contemporaries on the hills to the west, though nothing has quite the impact as the huge fort on Yeavering Bell, 927293, a mile from the road near Kirknewton. A mere 1,182ft (360m), and quite easy to climb, this is one of the most rewarding of Northumbrian hills for views. A wall of tumbled grey stones amid the encroaching heather and bilberry encloses an area of 17 acres (7ha) where the foundations of 130 circular huts have been identified. Clearly this must have been the main stronghold, or oppidum, for a large area of pre-Roman Celts. Looking down from its ramparts, and beyond the foot of the steep hill, fields now hide the remains of the royal palace of Gefrin, home of Saxon kings. The fertile landscape is largely one of eighteenth and nineteenth century enclosures, farms, woodlands and shelter-belts. Medieval castles dot the distant coast, and nearer pele-towers echo in smaller scale the troubled centuries before 1600. Vision spans 2,500 years of man in Northumbria in a single view in which there is scarcely a discordant note.

Excavation on Yeavering Bell suggests that many of the huts were of timber, but, like so many hill-top settlements, the basic form seems to have extended over centuries, probably until the end of the Roman occupation, although their defensible nature had long been unnecessary. Indeed, settlements of a similar structure, but at much lower levels, have been identified elsewhere in the Cheviot foothills, concentrated in three main groups – around the Breamish valley, on the southern flank of the Happy Valley south of Wooler, and above the feeders of the Bowmont and the Glen, especially west of Yeavering.

The common factor of these settlements seems to be an oval forecourt or stockyard. At Lordenshaw and Alnham Castlehill, settlements sprawl across older ones more defensive in nature. Greaves Ash, 965163, above Linhope at the head of the Breamish valley, is the largest group of this type, suggesting expansion over a period of time. Indeed, it has been described as 'the largest accretion of huts and courtyards in the whole county'. In one group there are the foundations of twenty-seven stone huts, and thirteen in another 100yd (89m) away. Single enclosure walls are 6ft (1.8m) thick. The huts themselves varied from 12-27ft (3.6-8.3m), with an average of 20ft (6m), and associated courtyards may have been paved or cobbled. Over 4sq miles (2.5sq km) of the Breamish valley, 150 stone-founded huts have been identified, together with a number of field systems, on Knock Hill, Meggrin's Knowe and East Hartside. These homes were characteristic of the area of the Celtic tribes called Votadini who were widely but loosely dispersed over north Northumberland by the time of the Roman conquest of the north. They are also probably the last form of small settlement observable on the ground before the establishment of much more recent farmsteads. Although these undefended native settlements are especially common in the Cheviot foothills, in frequently sheltered situations on lee slopes with a south-easterly aspect, they are not necessarily confined to this area. To the south of the Simonside Hills and north of Hadrian's Wall, though fewer in number they tend to be rectilinear rather than oval, and favour lower-lying sites on riverside spurs. In the valley of the North Tyne examples of such sites occur at Riding Wood, west of Bellingham, 818846, and in woodland at Sidwood on the Tarset Burn, 774894.

## The Roman Occupation

When the Romans crossed the Tyne shortly before AD80 they entered the tribal territory extending northwards to the Firth of Forth of the Votadini, colourfully described by Professor Sir Ian Richmond as a race of 'Celtic cowboys, footloose and unpredictable, moving with their animals and herds over rough pastures and moorland'. Establishing forts and bases at Corbridge (Corstopitum) and Chesterholm (Vindolanda), linked by the supply route of the Stanegate, Agricola pushed his main military route northwards along the line of what became Dere Street, with further forts at High Rochester (Bremenium) and Chew Green on the high Cheviot ridge. A second route branched off, a few miles north of Corbridge, aligned on the mouth of the Tweed. Later called the Devil's Causeway, its course has been traced, though is not now visible on the ground. At Low Learchild, *093112*, it met a branch from High Rochester.

By about AD84 Agricola had reached as far north in Scotland as the Spey valley, but he himself was recalled soon afterwards. Around AD87 the Romans withdrew from Scotland north of the Forth-Clyde isthmus, and within the next twenty years had abandoned southern Scotland. The Stanegate between Newcastle and Carlisle became the frontier, and after a probable British revolt the Emperor Hadrian visited Britain. Almost immediately plans were made and work started on what was to become the northern frontier of the vast Roman empire.

Hadrian's Wall is the most imposing surviving memorial in Europe to Roman military power, for nowhere else is there such a system of visible fortifications. Of its 73 miles (117km) across the narrowest part of England, fifteen are within the National Park, and these include the best-preserved sections, together with forts, milecastles, turrets, temples, bath-houses and milestones; while for about seven miles the Park's southern boundary follows the line of the Stanegate. Unlike many Roman sites in Britain, Hadrian's Wall can hardly fail to stir the imagination, if only because of the sheer magnitude of the undertaking. It epitomises the arrogant confidence of the regime that conceived it, as well as the organisational resources needed to build and maintain it for about 300 years. Quite simply, it is a monumental piece of civil engineering allied to the uniquely defensive nature of much of the course it adopted.

The Whin Sill cuesta was tailor-made for a barrier such as a raised patrol-route which the Wall was planned to be. Abundant supplies of good stone were readily available, and there was no shortage of native labour. The nearby Stanegate was a splendid supply route, protected by Agricola's early forts. As originally planned, the Wall was to be over fifteen feet high and ten feet wide, faced with well-shaped stone and in-filled with puddled earth and clay. Milecastles were introduced every Roman mile (1,620yd, 1,480m) to house patrolling troops with two equidistant turrets 540yd (494m) apart between each pair of milecastles used as signalling towers. Many of these vanished during the restoration of the Wall in the third century, but a number of well-preserved milecastles have survived, one of the best being No 42 at Cawfields, north of Haltwhistle, *715666*, with walls 8ft (2.4m) thick and seven or eight courses high enclosing a rectangle 63 x 49ft (19.2 x

*Milecastle 42 and the Roman wall at Cawfields Crag, looking west to the water-filled Cawfields Quarry*

14m), with large gateways on the northern and southern sides. Milecastles like this would have housed thirty to fifty men for patrol and sentry duty, while the intervening turrets, about 14ft sq (4.2m), housed four men.

Shortly after work was started on the Wall it was decided to move the main fighting force from its positions on the Stanegate northwards to the Wall itself, where it would be housed in a series of sixteen forts between 3 and 7 miles apart (4.8 and 11.2km). About the same time it was decided to narrow the Wall from 10 to 8ft (3 to 2.4m), to extend it eastwards from Newcastle to Wallsend, and to replace the 5 mile stretch of turf wall west of the River Irthing with one of stone, although it was almost forty years before this was completed. Most of the forts projected southwards from the Wall, but on cliff edges were constructed parallel to it. Larger forts about 5 acres (2ha) in extent housed about 1,000 infantry or 500 cavalry, and smaller ones about half this size. Within them were barrack-blocks, the commandant's house, a colonnaded headquarters, granaries to carry a year's supply of corn, workshops and latrines. Outside each fort was a suite of baths, temples and shrines, and a civil village where garrison wives might live, together with other civilians concerned with supplying various needs for the military personnel.

Except where the north-facing crags of the Whin Sill made it unnecessary, a Ditch, 27ft wide and 9ft deep (8.2 x 2.9m), accompanies the Wall on its northern side, while 60-80yd (55-73m) south of the Wall a far more impressive ditch, the Vallum, follows a parallel but straighter course. Mounds of excavated soil along each side of the Vallum make the whole earthwork about 120yd (110m) across, representing at least a million man-days of digging. It formed the southern edge of the military zone, a civilian customs-barrier. Between it and the Wall ran the Military Way linking forts, milecastles and turrets, a 20ft (6m) wide metalled road constructed for the rapid movement of troops to combat any attack from the north against a salient of the Wall. Today, a succession of field-gates across miles of farm tracks mark its course.

A labour force of 10,000 men took eight years to build the Wall. When, last century the historian Collingwood Bruce asked a builder friend to cost it at 1850 prices, the estimate was £1 million, plus about £50,000 for the Ditch and Vallum. If it were built today in reinforced concrete the cost would probably be near £200 million, a sum which enables us perhaps to grasp the financial burden its construction placed on Rome's exchequer.

The Wall was built to last as the fixed northern frontier of Rome, the last grasp of the imperial power. It would keep out the Votadini, the Celtic Picts, and it would keep in the Brigantes of northern England. The Wall's garrison was withdrawn in AD196 because of civil war on the continent, and some of the Wall's defences were breached and broken. About ten years later they were repaired, to remain intact for the next 150 years, and in spite of further raids, continued to be serviceable until the early years of the fifth century when the last Roman garrisons were finally withdrawn from Britain. The Wall had known 275 years of usefulness, garrisoned and patrolled by eight to ten generations of Roman military personnel.

St Cuthbert may have been the Wall's first tourist in 685 when he visited Carlisle and saw its Roman walls. Twelve centuries of local plundering since then have removed enormous quantities of dressed stone, leaving only about 10 miles (16km) of worthwhile sections in the middle, roughly between Sewingshields, 812703, in the east and Thirlwall, 660661, in the west, with the best sections in the eastern half of this, say from Cawfields Milecastle, 715666, to Housesteads fort, 789688. Although much can be seen from the Military Road, the B6318, nothing can match the experience, the exuberance, of walking along the Wall itself, savouring its wild and windy miles, with history beneath your boots.

At four of the main forts open to the public you can see and compare different aspects of life in this northern outpost of Rome. At Corstopitum, a mile from Corbridge, Agricola built the first fort to guard

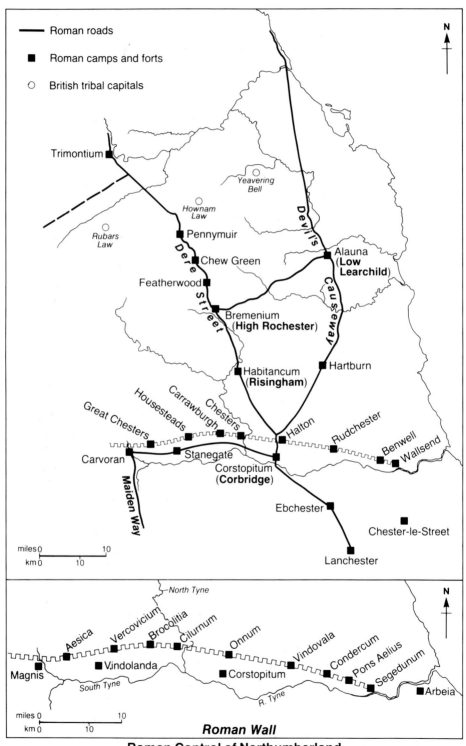

**Roman Control of Northumberland**

the important river crossing nearby, and it subsequently became the supply-base for his advance northwards. The remains of a large storehouse, granaries, compounds, houses and shops, even a strong-room, express in the eloquence of stone walls and foundations the importance of Corstopitum, not only in Agricola's campaign but in the later plan for Hadrian's Wall, so dependent on the Stanegate which passed east-west through the centre of the fort.

Chesters, which the Romans called Cilurnum, on the west bank of the North Tyne at Chollerford, housed one of the Wall's few cavalry garrisons. People have been visiting it for centuries, and it was John Clayton, Newcastle's Town Clerk 1822–67, a close friend of Dobson and Grainger, who owned the Chesters estate and initiated scientific excavation and preservation of much of the fort, as well as of the bridge abutments at the riverside. The parkland setting conceals the extensive lay-out, and although there is not a great deal to see above ground the museum is a treasure-house of finds. The baths are separate from the fort, nearer the river; an impressive complex of linked rooms illustrating the extent to which bathing was a Roman fetish for both soldiers and civilians, although the authorities were even then frowning on the mixed bathing which apparently occurred.

Three miles (5km) west of Chesters, in a field south of the road, was the fort of Brocolitia, of which nothing survives. However, in the dry summer of 1949, adjoining the known site of the fort, a Mithraic Temple was discovered, almost by accident, and excavation brought to light three altar-stones. These are now in the Museum of Antiquities at Newcastle, and three copies replace them in their original setting, open to the grey northern sky, their inscriptions glorifying Roman gods. Coventina's Well nearby, opened by Clayton in 1876, yielded over 13,000 coins and a wide range of other small objects, votive offerings to those same distant gods.

Five miles west again (8km) an enormous roadside car-park signifies the nearness of Housesteads, the best Roman fort on the Wall, and a mainly uphill half-mile (0.8km) walk from the road. Dramatic in its setting beneath the Whin Sill's crest, exposed to the elements, it looks – and was – a true frontier fort, seen at its best on a crisp winter's day, with grass bleached, stones stark, peopled only by the cold ghosts of cohorts past. Regular excavation since 1838 has yet uncovered only about half of the 3-acre (1.2ha) site, but there's plenty to appreciate, especially the headquarters building, the granaries, and, in the south-east corner, the latrines, Britain's best Roman loo, a reminder of this basic necessity of civilised life fourteen centuries ago on a draughty Northumbrian hillside.

The 3-mile (5km) walk westwards from Vercovicium along the turf-topped Wall, with the wind in your face and cloud-shadows racing across the uplands is a memorable march along England's oldest frontier. Names of landscape features stamp out the rhythm of centuries: Hotbank Crags, Crag Lough, Cuddy's Crag, Peel Crag; curlew-call, plaint of plover, jackdaw's clack, and sheep-voices borne along the wind, the same sounds and sights as those known to Roman patrols.

A couple of miles south-west of Housesteads, and on the line of the Stanegate, Chesterholm offers a different experience. At the fort of Vindolanda – not a Wall fort but part of an earlier defence system guarding the route of the Stanegate through the Tyne gap – Professor Eric Birley and his son Robin established the Vindolanda Trust in 1969, with the main aims of excavation and interpretative display. Additionally, it provides facilities for training youngsters in archaeological excavation, and, using such youthful enthusiasm, has channelled it into interesting reconstructions. One of these involved the rebuilding, within Roman limitations and conditions, of a full-sized replica of a section of Roman Wall complete with milecastle and timber turret. The result is impressively convincing. Part of the Vindolanda site was a civilian settlement, or vicus, the only one on the Wall's length which is now being excavated. One of Vindolanda's fascinations is that history is constantly being revealed, and new methods of display are being explored. The Stanegate here is splendidly revealed, and in a quiet grove to the east of the fort stands a massive Roman milestone, probably the only one in Britain surviving in situ to its original height, and there is the stump of another one a Roman mile to the west, on the normal approach to Vindolanda.

If it is the Wall and its garrison forts that have attracted the archaeologists and continue to draw the crowds, it was the great road, Dere Street, slicing through the county, that represented the main thread of Roman presence in the past. Along it were the marching-camps of Roman troops, fourteen identified in the 20 miles (32km) between the Scottish Border and Chesterhope Common south of Redesdale. Most are mere mounds in the grass, with little masonry, but at High Rochester, or Bremenium, 833986, 'the place of the roaring stream', the stone remains are more extensive than at any other British site north of Hadrian's Wall. Indeed, after the last withdrawal from Scotland about AD213 Bremenium was the most northerly fort in the Roman Empire, and was finally abandoned in AD343, having seen just over 200 years of occupation. A few courses of masonry outline parts of its walls, massive jambs indicate positions of gateways, and a six foot wall was part of an internal tower. By the side of Dere Street, 750yd (685m) south-east of the fort, two courses of massive masonry mark the remains of a monumental tomb, probably of a high-ranking officer. The former schoolhouse in Rochester village has a number of Roman gutter-stones built into its porch, together with two stone balls used in a catapult.

Many lonely miles to the north, almost on the Border as it strides the

The copies of the three Roman altar-stones excavated from the Mithraic Temple at Brocolitia. The actual altar-stones are now in the Museum of Antiquities, Newcastle, and these copies are displayed in their original setting. (below) The famous latrines at Housesteads Fort

Cheviot ridge, 1,400ft (427m) up in a world of skylark-song and wind-blown grasses, Chew Green surely epitomises Roman determination. The ground-plan of two vast rectangular camps, incongruous in their isolation, well justify Sir Nikolaus Pevsner's description as 'the most remarkable visible group of Roman earthworks in Britain'. You approach them best from Coquetdale, by a mile walk beyond the last farm at Makendon, along the metalled army road and then by a grassy track.

At the opposite end of the county, above the South Tyne near Alston, Whitley Castle's situation is one of Pennine grandeur, 695488. Although no masonry is visible the system of seven banks and ditches protecting its vulnerable south-western flank, and its north-western and south-eastern ramparts, make it remarkably impressive. Little of its history is known, but it is thought to have been built in the second century, possibly to guard the important lead-mines on nearby hills and the important route, the Maiden Way, linking the Vale of Eden with the Stanegate and the Wall near Greenhead. The fort is only a few minutes' walk from the A689, but you are advised to ask permission to visit it at Whitlow Farm. The Pennine Way passes close to the eastern side of Whitley Castle.

## The Early English

After the Wall was abandoned and Roman military and civil control withdrawn by the first decade of the fifth century the Northumbrian uplands probably were left to the thinly-scattered tribes of the existing Celtic kingdoms. Nothing of certainty is known about any permanent settlement for at least the next two centuries, but by the middle of the sixth century an Anglian kingdom was beginning to be established, embracing all land between the Humber and the Forth. The northern kingdom, Bernicia, was based on Bamburgh, the southern one, Deira, based on York. It is from Deira that the name of the Roman spine road, Dere Street, originated. The new kingdom was Northumbria, but the colonising Angles favoured arable farming, for which the uplands north of the Wall were unsuited, so they continued to be occupied by a Celtic-speaking population, whose homesteads were timber and of which nothing survives.

By the end of the sixth century Anglian expansion westwards reached the foot of the Cheviots, and it is known that by then the royal palace of Edwin (583–633) was in existence at Yeavering, 925305. Excavations of its site suggest that this was based on a large timbered hall. Again, nothing survives above ground, but by the side of the road (A697) near the farm of Old Yeavering, west of Wooler, an enclave of modern walling incorporates a neatly-lettered plaque: 'At this place was Gefrin, royal township of the seventh-century Anglo-Saxon Kings of Northumbria. Here the missionary Paulinus in AD627 instructed the people in

Christianity for thirty-six days and baptised them in the River Glen close by'. This information comes from Bede's writings of almost a century later. If they are to be accepted as factual they imply a considerable population scattered around the Glendale area.

Place-name evidence is not necessarily reliable, but one of the earliest forms of Anglo-Saxon place names includes the elements '–ingham'. A few miles south-east of Wooler are Chillingham, Eglingham, Edlingham and Whittingham, small villages in vale country where an arable cultivation could be followed. Bellingham, in the North Tyne valley, points to advancing settlement along the broad valleys farther south. But in the hill country Celtic place-names abound, particularly in river names – Aln, Breamish, Coquet, Till, Tweed, Tyne and Wansbeck, together with Kielder.

It seems probable that, although there were no clear-cut boundaries on the land, Anglo-Saxon villages and hamlets favoured the lower country away from the hill-margins, the uplands themselves were not suited to Anglo-Saxon farmers, and Celtic settlement in the form of scattered farmsteads and small hamlets survived, in North Tynedale, Redesdale and Coquetdale above Hepple. There is no typical village or hamlet, and while it might be satisfying to think that the shapes of some settlements, the greens at Elsdon and Wall for instance, may recall earlier times, three centuries of later unrest, with many places laid waste will probably have changed the scene considerably.

Anglo-Saxon sculpture and churches provide further evidence for the pattern of settlement before the Conquest. Early Celtic Christianity was based on the monastery, from which missionary monks travelled far and wide preaching the Gospel and performing various church ceremonies. Traces of a Celtic church were revealed in the Yeavering royal palace, but it was not until the end of the seventh century that stone churches made their appearance. St Wilfrid's church at Hexham, surviving today in the crypt of the later Priory church, was sensitively described by Pevsner as 'perhaps the most moving monument in medieval Northumberland'. Hexham was established as a monastic community in the late seventh century, by when the Northumbrian landscape had acquired a framework of settlement which has formed the basis of what we see today. Under the northern king, Oswy, who died in 641, conditions of relative peace contributed to a slow growth in population, so that individuals and small groups moved out into new territories, creating their own hams, tons, and dons.

Elsdon may be 'Elli's dene or valley', Kidland in upper Coquetdale was almost certainly 'Cydda's land', and Rothbury was 'Hropa's burgh'. The first element of the family name here is particularly interesting: try to pronounce the 'Hr' by rolling the 'r', and you produce that quirky peculiarity of the Northumbrian 'r' which makes it sound like part of a gargle, something that Defoe noticed in the 1720s, and which has provoked discussion ever since. Northumbrian dialect is related to 'Northern Inglis' which probably originated in the Anglo-Saxon kingdom of Bernicia, based on Bamburgh. Although this embraced all the land from Humber to Forth, the Northern Inglis dialect gradually separated itself from the Scottish Lowland Anglo-Saxon, a process strengthened by the later three hundred years of Anglo-Scottish wars. The Lowland Anglo-Saxon became accepted as the Scottish tongue north of the Tweed, while the Northern Inglis south of the Tweed became affected by Midland English. Thus, although there are dialect differences between the speech of Lowland Scots and native Northumbrians, they share common historic roots based on the Anglo-Saxon settlement. To visit one of the Northumbrian rural markets or Border shows and listen to the talk of the local farmers and shepherds is to journey backwards through time to the sounds of ancestral voices.

Anglian farmers preferred sites with some shelter, where good arable land with well-drained soils enabled them to plough and to grow their crops. They ventured to the margins of the hills, where tracks came down from the old hill-forts to the lower ground of the vales. Alwinton stands at the foot of Clennell Street, but the original site may have been at Low Alwinton, a short distance to the south, where St Michael's church now stands solitarily above the east bank of the Coquet, largely a nineteenth-century replacement of a much older building. Nearby is the site of a known deserted medieval village. Alwinton was the first of the 'Ten Towns of Coquetdale' – with Biddlestone, Clennell, Chirmundesden, Sharperton, Farnham, Burradon, Netherton, Fawdon and Ingram – all Anglian settlements, and most still the sites of farmsteads or hamlets.

Ingram was founded at the point where the River Breamish emerges from a confined valley to join the calmer landscape of Whittingham Vale. Its derivation from 'angr' meaning grassland, suggests that the smooth grassy hills were significant landscape features in Anglian times. Its church, too, is dedicated to St Michael, and contains some Norman masonry. Before the Conquest there may have been a simple wooden building here.

Fawdon is only a mile to the south-east, and Whittingham only 4 miles (6.4km) away, at a point where two fords cross the River Aln near where the Roman road to Berwick, the Devil's Causeway, is joined by the lateral Roman road from Dere Street at Low Learchild. Characteristic of Anglian settlement, however, it kept away from the Roman roads themselves, keeping them a mile distant. Well-drained soils of Cementstone country attracted a larger community than most in the area, and St Bartholomew's church contains some impressive Saxon masonry in the lower parts of its tower and in the quoins at the eastern end of the nave. More is the pity that the upper half of the tower was deliberately demolished in the 1840s, in order to build a taller Gothic addition.

Over large areas of the countryside the population was widely scattered, and there was no provision for a resident priest. Occasionally, to provide a meeting-place at which local folk could assemble for worship, preaching crosses were set up, and the finest date from the early years of Northumbrian Christianity. Undoubtedly the best is at Bewcastle, a few miles across the Cumbrian border beyond the western edge of the Forest Park, reached along remote, minor roads north-west from Gilsland. Probably of the late seventh century, its cross-shaft towers 14ft (4m) above the ground in the churchyard, its four faces throbbing with delicate carvings, vine scrolls, chequers, animals and sacred figures including St John the Evangelist, St John the Baptist with the Agnus Dei, and Christ stepping on a lion and an adder, a scroll in one hand and the other raised in blessing. Believed to be the work of Northumbrian monks, the Bewcastle cross is regarded as one of the two most perfect early Christian crosses in Europe (the other is at Ruthwell, Dumfries), well worth the effort of a long detour to see it.

In All Saints', Rothbury, the font is constructed from part of the shaft of a Saxon cross, probably of c800, although the bowl bears the date 1664. The shaft contains scroll work, animals and figures, rather harder in outline than those at Bewcastle. A group of Apostles is shown with the front figure holding a book, the usual Anglo-Saxon symbol of an evangelist. Other fragments of the cross, rescued from the demolition of the older church prior to its 1850 rebuilding are now in the Museum of Antiquities at·Newcastle.

# 3

# THE MEDIEVAL LANDSCAPE

During the eleventh century Northumberland enjoyed a period of comparative peace, during which, as we have seen, some churches were restored and new towns built, as at Corbridge and Whittingham. By the time of the Conquest the foundations of a feudal society had been laid, albeit under a northern earldom comprising a loose confederation of Celtic, Danish, Norse and Saxon settlements. Perhaps it was not surprising that William mistrusted them. In 1069 he moved rapidly to York to put down a northern rebellion, and as a reprisal, during the two years following this laid waste all the land between York and Durham, the worst genocide in English history in which according to one chronicler, 100,000 people perished. The crippled northern kingdom now lay at the mercy of the Scots. Northumberland became a deserted land, with every town except Bamburgh destroyed. William spent two weeks checking Border security before returning southwards through Coquetdale via Harbottle and Hexham. After subsequently defeating the Scottish King Malcolm, William imposed a strict control over northern England, introducing new taxes and demanding service from everyone.

He appointed a Norman earl of Northumberland to look after his interests, but over the troubled Border hills and valleys he relied on the known self-interest of his barons, granting them 'liberties' or franchises where the king's writ did not run, including those of Hexham and Redesdale, followed in the twelfth century by North and South Tynedale. The thinly-scattered population, averaging about one family to every 60 acres (24ha), owed military and personal service to these Norman overlords who by the time of Henry I (1100–1134) had begun to acquire estates, build castles and found religious houses.

The family of de Umfraville held the Liberty of Redesdale and upper Coquetdale, and although their main Northumbrian castle was at Prudhoe, in the Tyne valley, their headquarters in the Liberty was at Elsdon, which commanded two old and well-used routes between England and Scotland, one running by the Roman Dere Street from High Rochester to the Kale Water, crossing the Border above Chew Green, and the other following the course of the present A68, crossing the Border at the Redeswire (the neck or col of the River Rede). Elsdon was also relatively convenient to the Northumbrian lowlands of the Tyne valley east of Hexham.

The old castle, now called Mote Hill, is the best motte-and-bailey site in the county, an artificial earthwork on a spur above the ravine of the Elsdon Burn. The round motte is about 50ft (15m) high, and has a flat top 150ft (46m) across. Beyond the deep ditch on its north side a half-acre bailey is further protected by more earthen banks and ditches, while the ravine on the west enhances its invulnerability. Although the road to Rothbury, the B6341, passes between the earthwork and Elsdon Burn, a belt of trees obscures the view, so that the best impression of its situation and appearance is obtained from the minor road which leaves Elsdon and climbs south-eastwards on to the moors.

Ironically, as a result of the changed political climate under Henry II, Elsdon's fortress was replaced about 1157, after only forty or fifty years of importance, by another motte-and-bailey castle more strategically placed at Harbottle, in the upper Coquet valley. This, like its Elsdon predecessor, would initially have been largely timber-built, but the fragments of masonry walling which survive on its motte are probably of later date, when Harbottle was the keystone of the defences of the Middle March.

Wark-on-Tyne was the capital of the Liberty of Tynedale which comprised almost the whole of the two Tyne valleys north and west of Hexham, and there are meagre traces of a former motte-and-bailey castle still identifiable in a field called the Mote hill. The writs of the English king did not apply to Tynedale, and its inhabitants owed no military service to him, a situation that continued until 1296 when Edward I deprived John Balliol of his ownership of Tynedale. Famous families who flourished in Tynedale included Comyns, Whitfields, and Swinburnes (who still own estates there). John Comyn built Tarset Castle, 788855,

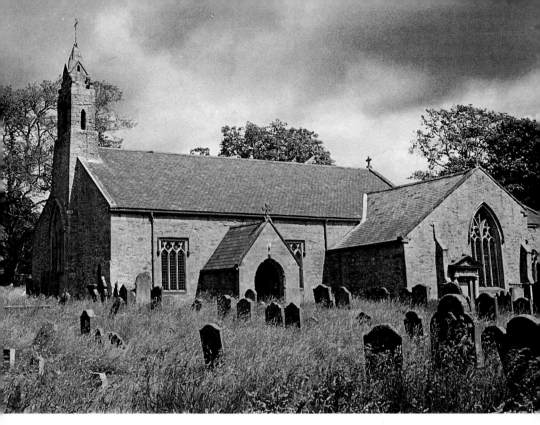

*St Cuthbert's Church, Elsdon*

about 1267 and David Lindsay the castle of Dally, little more than a mile away, thirty years earlier. Virtually nothing survives of either of these medieval strongholds.

The presence of the two large Liberties of Redesdale and Tynedale under their own powerful lords explains the absence of any large castles in the National Park area. The Crown held very little land in the county, and there were no other lords concerned with the uplands. North of the Coquet the Cheviot country was so remote and sparsely populated that there was no need for castles. However, 1296 saw an important change in the political and administrative conditions of north Northumberland. After a long period of peace, Edward I, tempted to meddle with the Scottish succession, declared war on Scotland, and for the next fifty years a very destructive warfare spread across both sides of the Border, with buildings destroyed, crops ruined, many men killed, hostages taken, ransoms demanded. Edward I instituted a system of government along the English side of the Border by the Wardens of the Marches, responsible for defence and the enforcement of Marcher Law. The northern parts of Northumberland and Cumberland became military zones, with Cumberland forming the West March, Northumberland the East March which, by the end of the fourteenth century, was subdivided. The new East March, comprising the coastal plain north of the

Aln, was based on Berwick, while the Middle March – the whole of the English Cheviots, Coquetdale, Redesdale and the North Tyne valley – was centred on Harbottle.

## Monasteries

Parallel with the strong, feudal influence of the baronies which controlled most of the landscape within the National Park area, the more benign effect of monastic landlords needs to be considered. In the four centuries following Domesday monasteries played a substantial part in the evolution of the landscape, although this was much less than in the Pennine dales of Yorkshire. In 1113 Hexham priory was refounded on the site of Wilfrid's great church by Augustinian canons, and in 1135 the lords of Mitford granted canons of the same Order land by the River Coquet east of Rothbury for the establishment of Brinkburn priory. The Brinkburn canons gradually brought into cultivation some of the high ground north of the Coquet between their monastery and Rothbury, and they were also granted the rights of clearing and ditching the road between Longframlington and over Thorny Hill, 410008, to Cragend, by the present B6344, and thence along the road to Rothbury.

In 1165 Walter de Bolbec founded Blanchland Abbey for Premonstratensian canons in the sparsely inhabited country near the head of the Derwent valley, on the southern edge of Hexhamshire. They soon cleared the woods to create the riverside haughs which exist above the attractive village today, and records show that they built a mill by the north-east corner of the present bridge. The white habit worn by the canons was similar to that of the Cistercian monks, and the village name probably derives from the same source.

It was a Cistercian house, Newminster, near Morpeth, founded in 1157 as the first daughter house of the great Fountains Abbey, whose monks played an important role in the evolution of Cheviot landscapes of upper Coquetdale. Newminster itself was destroyed by the Scots in the year it was completed, but it was rebuilt to become one of the largest Cistercian abbeys in northern England. Sadly, nothing but a few fragments remain of this great building – a few exposed foundations, some masonry, and a reconstructed small section of cloister arcading. However, among the huge estates which Newminster gradually acquired was much of upper Coquetdale, granted to them by the de Umfraville lords of Redesdale and Harbottle. From 1181 to the Dissolution in 1536 Newminster Abbey held the lordship of Kidland, with 17,000 acres of upland grazing north of the River Coquet. The fact that sheep could graze these vast pastures suggests that, by medieval times, the older wilderness had retreated and wolves were probably near to extinction.

In common with other Cistercian foundations, Newminster was a great producer of wool, and the monks' sheep farms were based on granges. Between these and the parent abbey near Morpeth there would have been constant movement of monastic officials, lay-brethren, livestock and wool. In 1228 the abbot and monks of Newminster entered into an agreement with Thomas of Clennell who granted wayleave for:

> their men and carts and flocks in going and coming through the vill of Clennel, going up the valley by the Alwin to Kidland, and also going to the east through the vill of Clennell, across the ditch, and so to the south across the head of the ploughed land to the east of the ditch as far as the Allerhope Burn. It was further agreed that if the monks' flocks and herds should feed in the Clennell pastures, payment should be made at the rate of 1d for twenty cattle, 1d for forty sheep, 4d for ten mares with a stallion, and 1d for mares without a stallion. Thomas was to pay at the same rate if his animals strayed into the monks' pasture.

This extract from the Newminster Chartulary helps to bring into sharper focus a picture of grazing flocks and herds on unenclosed pastures, straying a little from their domain, and having to be gathered from time to time by their shepherds who lived in lonely places. Some of the grazing was let to local farmers on the English side of the Border, but troubled times in the fourteenth and fifteenth centuries frequently caused a scarcity of such tenants, and a resultant decrease in rents, so that the monks themselves took over the stocking and management of their Coquetdale estates.

Kidland Burn and the River Alwin probably formed the eastern boundary of the Newminster lands, the boundary continuing north-westwards over Yarnspath Law, 888136, to Uswayford and the present Border line on the Cheviot watershed. The 'great road to Yarnspeth' named in the charter was Clennell Street, its course now partly enclosed within the dark plantations of Kidland Forest. However, the western boundary of the lordship retains its more open, original character, and can be followed from Rowhopeburnsmouth, 860114, north-westwards on to the ridge by Hindside Knowe, 847120, where the map names the track as 'The Street', to Black Braes and the Border line west of Windy Gyle.

On the north bank of the Coquet opposite Windyhaugh, 866110, the monks had a fulling-mill, whose foundations were, early last century, still existent. The doorhead of an old house at Windyhaugh may have come from the mill. Its unusual porphyritic stone bears the inscription I^BC 1760, representing the Georgian rebuilding of an older property, by James Burn and his wife Catherine.

*Blanchland, framed in the archway of the former priory gatehouse (c1500). The houses were built for lead miners c1752*

Two miles north of Shillmoor, in the narrow, steep-sided valley of the Usway Burn, at about 900ft (275m) the shepherd's house of Batailshiel Haugh was referred to in the thirteenth century Newminster chartulary as the 'shiel or summer farmstead of Henry de Bataile', who himself later gave one Henry Carpenter a site at the mouth of the Ridlees Burn, a mile below Shillmoor, now occupied by Linshiels. At nearby Quickening Cote the broad area of riverside haughs were owned in 1317 by a Richard Horsley. Thus is seen in the Coquet valley, and in its remote tributary valleys, a continuity of settlement and land use covering at least seven centuries.

The name Linshiels, incorporating the Norse element, 'shiels', meaning 'summer pastures', suggests a far more ancient settlement. During medieval times transhumance was a common practice in the north country pastoral farming, being the seasonal movement of flocks and herds, with their shepherds, from winter pastures to summer ones. The temporary huts occupied during summer months were called shielings, usually stone-built with two small rooms, and roofed with turf. None has survived complete, but some can be identified as ruins or just foundations, while others have been replaced by later buildings on the same site. They are not confined to Coquetdale, but occur in Redesdale and North Tynedale where the National Park Authority have identified forty specific sites. In those areas shielings continued in use until the eighteenth century, when more peaceful conditions allied to more efficient methods of managing pastures, through enclosures, made permanent settlement possible.

On the south-eastern slopes of Cushat Law, in the junction between the Sting and Yoke Burns, now almost hidden by tussocky grass, Memmerkirk may have been a shieling, or even a medieval long house. Excavation in the early 1960s revealed the footings of a stone walled building 46ft (14m) long by nearly 16ft (4.9m) wide, divided into three unequal bays, and with a possible extension running the length of the rear, north wall. Fourteenth-century pottery dated it to the period of monastic ownership of Newminster, but, in spite of its name, there is no conclusive evidence that it was a chapel. Nearby, on the ridge between Cushat Law and Hogdon Law, near Sting Head, now afforested, stood one of a number of stone crosses mentioned by Hodgson last century as being on the trackway between Alwinton and Ingram. Since it has long since vanished we cannot say whether it was a guide to travellers, or a boundary stone on the edge of the Newminster lands.

Brinkburn Priory had a small estate at Puncherton, 935095, north of Clennell, while on the northern side of the Cheviot watershed, among the hills to the west of the College valley, land at Trowupburn was given to the Cistercian monks of Melrose Abbey in the early thirteenth century. Hexham Abbey owned extensive estates in Hexhamshire, and

*The North Door of Brinkburn Priory, showing the exuberant late-Norman ornament*

the names of some of the present-day farms in West Allendale may be significant, in particular Monk, 783565, with Westside and Burnlaw nearby. It is known that farms were established in these wild areas during medieval times by 'the enclosure and clearance of rough land by individuals who were accepted as manorial tenants by the Abbey, mainly on copyhold tenure'. This was a tenure dependent on custom and the will of the lord of the manor, and usually carried certain obligations to perform services for the lord, but following the Black Death (c1350) and the resultant scarcity of labour these services were commuted to money payments. Tenants were protected by title written into manorial court-rolls.

Although the four northern counties were excluded from the Domesday survey it has been established that the population of Northumberland then averaged 5.4 persons per square mile, a very low figure compared with Devon's 23.1 and Norfolk's 42.5. Even nine centuries ago, the greater proportion was concentrated in the county's south-eastern corner, leaving the uplands very sparsely populated indeed. The peaceful conditions which prevailed between about 1150 and 1300 encouraged economic expansion and the resultant colonisation of many areas of land hitherto considered waste, a state of affairs which was not confined to Northumberland, but which took place all over Europe. It seems probable that over much of the county the various new 'hams', 'tons' and 'steads' came into existence during the second half of the twelfth century and the first half of the thirteenth. Indeed, in the upland regions and along the fringes of the hills it is likely that, at the eve of the Scottish wars around 1300, settlement had reached a 'high noon', not to be regained until the middle of the eighteenth century, if at all.

Newtown, 036007, on the lower northern slopes of the Simonside Hills, was founded, as Rothbury Newtown, between 1214 and 1240. Above its farmlands the boundary walls of the Norman lord's deer park still show traces in the heather and bracken. Some of the moorland waste and scrub of Rothbury Forest was also brought under cultivation at this time. At the head of the Coquet valley there was medieval settlement among the grass-covered embankments and enclosures of the Roman fort at Chew Green.

South of the Tyne between Hexham and Corbridge the burgesses of Corbridge, who had common rights on Corbridge Fell, granted Thomas of Devilstone twenty acres of waste and pasture on the fell, 'with liberty to enclose, dyke, hedge and empark', but he was not to plough any land. Today's Park Wood, above the Devil's Water, was once part of the medieval forest granted to Dilston (Develstone) at the end of the thirteenth century.

As the new settlements began to use up all the available land for ploughing and the sowing of crops, marginal land on the lower slopes of

the hills became taken in, and cultivated, as terraces now referred to as
lynchets. Most of these follow the contours along hillsides. Rarely less
than 55yd (50m) long, they were quite commonly 160-220yd (150-
200m), often occurring in series, one above another, called flights. After
first removing surface boulders and using these to form a step, or riser, on
the edge of the terrace, it was levelled out by ploughing to create what
was in effect a long field up to 16ft (5m) wide, tailing off at each end into
unploughed land. Lynchets are usually on the south-facing slopes of hills,
and throughout the Border uplands almost certainly date from the
century and a half of 'land hunger' prior to the Scottish wars.

Good examples of 'cultivation terraces', as they are marked on the
1:25,000 map, occur on hillsides to the south-west of Ingram, above the
Middleton Burn. To the north, above High Humbleton, west of Wooler,
the 1:25,000 map shows lynchets on the lower slopes of Humbleton Hill,
973283, marking the characteristic outlines of medieval ploughing. One
of the most familiar flights of lynchets is that crossing the civilian
settlement immediately to the south of the Roman fort at Housesteads. In
the far northern salient of the National Park, above Hethpool in the
College valley, numerous flights of cultivation terraces, named on the
1:50,000 map, furrow the steep southern slopes above the Elsdon Burn,
ideally seen in late afternoon or evening sunlight from the Iron Age
settlement on Little Hetha, 886280. Those on White Hill behind
Hethpool are conspicuous in the view from the valley road.

By the end of the thirteenth century, the population of
Northumberland had probably reached a peak, and by implication the
extent of arable land had grown to its greatest extent. In the Cheviots
cultivation had reached the 1,000ft (305m) contour, yet within a few
decades this high tide of settlement and cultivation had begun to recede,
slowly at first as the economy declined, but with accelerating pace after
Bannockburn (1314) and the Black Death (1348). There was a retreat
from the hills, particularly near the Border with its increasing hostility.
Thus, outlying villages, settled only the previous century or two, were
abandoned, and vast areas of ploughland returned to grass.

## Deserted Villages

Sites of deserted or shrunken medieval villages have been located over
the greater part of Northumberland. Of the 165 named in the 1968 list
produced by the DMV Research Group only five occur either south of the
Tyne or in Tynedale itself. The greatest concentration lies in the central
uplands between the North Tyne and the Wansbeck, now important
grazing country, but there is a handful in Redesdale around Otterburn,
several in Coquetdale between Rothbury and Alwinton, others in the
upper parts of the Aln and Breamish valleys, and a few more to the west of

Wooler. Abandonment of sites continued, for various reasons, until the nineteenth century, but here we are concerned only with the depopulation from the fourteenth century until the end of the Tudor period and the Union of the Crowns.

Evidence of abandoned former villages, seen on the ground particularly in the low-angle sunlight of winter, or early and late in the day, and impressively recorded by aerial photography, is the ridge-and-furrow of medieval ploughing which, fossilised through centuries of grazing, produces a corduroy pattern on the landscape. On Haystack Hill, near Ingram, 006151, such 'ridge-and-furrow' surrounds the remains of a former Romano-British settlement, and other good examples can be seen above the Breamish valley, north of Hartside, 985176, to the south above Alnhammoor, 965153, and on Leafield Edge, from the upland track between Alnhammoor and Alnham.

Sometimes more than the grassy corrugations of former ridge-and-furrow survive. In the Coquet valley, north-east of Harbottle, Chirmundesden was once one of the 'ten towns of Coquetdale', lonely in an upland setting where the green rounded hills of the southern Cheviot curve round to meet the dark crags south of Coquet. A survey of 1604 noted it as 'sometime a township', and it is thought to have disappeared during the previous century. Two tracks meet near its site, 950063, but only a few tumbled stones and mounds, the remains of former crofts, now mark the place where buildings stood, and medieval people lived. A few miles to the east and south-east, Burradon, Sharperton and Farnham, prosperous-looking farms today, occupy sites of other Coquetdale townships, while at Wreighill, 977020, above the junction of the Coquet and Grasslees Burn, more faint foundations mark the site of a small village which developed round a Cistercian grange of Newminster Abbey. Local tradition blames the depopulation here on the 1665 plague, but the settlement was already in decline as early as 1377. At Fallowfield, 930685, a mile east of the North Tyne valley near the Roman Wall, a single farm has now replaced the medieval village abandoned in late Tudor times, its site identified by low mounds surrounded by the ridge-and-furrow among the rough pasture and thicket nearby.

Next to nothing is known of the circumstances which caused settlements to be abandoned. However, marginal land at the frontiers of viable farming would have been most vulnerable to even small deteriorations in the climate. It is known that, from the late thirteenth century, mean summer temperatures started to decline, and winters became more severe. Fourteenth-century chroniclers recorded very bad winter storms, and after a brief improvement in the climate soon after 1500, there was a marked slump into what has been referred to as the Little Ice Age which lasted from 1600 until about 1750.

*Aydon Castle, above Corbridge*

Recent research into depopulation in the Lammermuir Hills of southern Scotland – about forty miles north of the Cheviots, and therefore climatically rather similar – suggests that a number of medieval villages probably vanished in the sixteenth and early seventeenth centuries. Thus it seems that worsening climate may have been a significant factor in the desertion of small villages on the Cheviot foothills above the Vale of Till and the Coquet, and that such abandonment may have occurred quite quickly. It would have needed only one bad year and its poor crops to necessitate additional livestock slaughter in the autumn. A peasant family would have eaten some of their seed-corn in the winter, leaving less to sow. A second bad summer would be near-disaster, and it would be doubtful if the suffering family would survive a second severe winter. They could quite literally have starved to death. In other cases, desertion of marginal settlements may have been more gradual, but the end result was the same, and it was one which left its indelible mark on the land in the pattern of corduroy ridge-and-furrow, and the long strip lynchets terracing the grassy hillsides well above the limits of arable farming carried on in the kinder climate of present times.

If such landscapes reveal the retreat from the frontiers of arable farming from the fourteenth to sixteenth centuries, it is the legacy of fortified buildings which so starkly illustrate the three centuries of regression arising from the continued strife with the Scots, from 1296 until the Union of the Crowns in 1603. Poverty, allied to insecure conditions of life in the Border area, has ensured that no peasant building from earlier than the seventeenth century survives in rural Northumberland. Indeed, according to some travellers who ventured so far north in the late eighteenth century, such peasant building as existed then was extremely primitive. In Hexham, along the South Tyne, and in Allendale, stone houses were being built, however, in the seventeenth century.

*The Coquet Valley above Alwinton*

# 4
# NEW BUILDINGS, NEW LANDSCAPES

When William Hutchinson travelled from Wooler to the Scottish Border in 1776 he wrote that 'the cottages of the lower class of people are deplorable, composed of upright timbers fixed in the ground, the interstices wattled and plastered with mud, some thatched and others covered with turf . . . a hearth stone on the ground for the peat and turf fire'. They must have differed scarcely at all from the crude huts in which Northumbrian peasants had lived in the Middle Ages. During the troubled centuries of Border warfare such buildings would have been regularly burnt, and as regularly rebuilt, but by the end of the eighteenth century and in the early years of last century they were being replaced by improving landlords. By the second half of the nineteenth century stone, slate and pantiles were being commonly used throughout the whole of Northumberland for these rebuilt farms and the humbler dwellings of labourers and shepherds. In the upland regions of this survey it is these structures which are most numerous, but in terms of architecture it is the older fortified buildings which are most striking; indeed, among all the English counties the northern parts of Northumberland and Cumbria stand supreme in their heritage of pele towers and bastle-houses.

The distinction here is one of degree. Three centuries of Border strife necessitated the building, by those who could afford to do so, of fortified homes. Rich and powerful families retired into the safety of their great castles, although no new castles were built in the upland areas during this time, as invading armies from Scotland invariably by-passed the hills, and entered Northumberland across the Tweed on the east, or from the west, via Cumberland and the Tyne Gap.

Lesser gentry built themselves tower-houses which have now become known as peles, while farmers in the remote uplands and their valleys occupied bastle-houses. To be strictly accurate the term 'pele' originally referred to the defensive enclosure in which they stood. When Henry V made a list of such towers in 1415, it included over eighty, among them some of the vicars' peles still standing, and still in use today.

*Alwinton Show*

The term 'bastle-house' needs more explanation. Sixteenth- and seventeenth-century documents show that it was used for peles and other strongly-built houses, and possibly for houses of sturdy timber construction enclosed within an earthen bank. Bastles were sometimes referred to as 'peles', or 'stone houses' by contemporary writers, but by now 'peles' are generally taken to be tower-houses, and 'bastle-houses' are defensible farmhouses, invariably rectangular in plan, with external dimensions of about 35 by 25ft (10.5 by 7.5m), of two full storeys, with steeply-pitched gables. The distribution of both types of fortified structures was governed by geographical and political factors. Peles are most commonly found in nucleated villages and hamlets on the edges of the hills and along the river valleys, and are far more widely distributed than bastle-houses, which tend to be much more a feature of scattered upland settlement.

With a few exceptions, surviving examples of bastle-houses occur within about twenty miles of the Border; indeed their southernmost limit of distribution runs so closely parallel with it that this cannot be regarded as mere coincidence. This distance is significant, for an Act of 1555 which required castles and forts to be repaired, and open ground enclosed with ditches and quick-set hedges in order to impede raiders' movements, referred to buildings within this distance. In 1584, Border Commissioners made a similar recommendation, and stipulated the same distance.

Additionally, within the area where bastles occur they tend to be sited in clusters, or at least within easy reach of their neighbours. At Gatehouse, 788889, in the valley of the Tarset Burn a few miles north-west of Bellingham, two bastle-houses face each other on opposite sides of the road, with a third across the valley at Redheugh, 600yd (550m) away. That on the north side of the road is one of the best-preserved bastles in the whole area and probably dates from the late sixteenth century. A mile farther up the valley, Black Middens Bastle-House, 774900, has been partially restored and made safe by English Heritage, and is freely open. Although roofless, its situation in a remote upland valley a few miles from the Border, and its structure give a vivid impression of the harsh reality of farm life on England's northern frontier four centuries ago.

Walls of large blocks of irregularly shaped stone are four feet thick on the ground floor and only a little less at first floor level. Ground-floor doors on the front are later insertions, the only entrance for cattle and other stock being by the doorway in the east gable. The only other openings on the ground floor are ventilation slits. Entrance to the upper floor, where the farming family lived, was through a doorway reached by a retrievable wooden ladder, later replaced by an outside stone stair. Massive stones forming the jambs of this doorway are characteristic of

*Gatehouse Bastle, a late sixteenth-century fortified farmhouse in the valley of the Tarset Burn*

those in other bastle-houses, and these have rebates for two harr-hung doors secured by heavy oak drawbars housed in small tunnels in the walls. Upper-floor windows are small, with surrounds of large stones, and a fireplace in the gable farthest from the doorway still shows smoke-blackening on the masonry above.

Black Middens Bastle-House had its upper floor supported on stout timber beams, closely set and spanning the width of the building. Some bastle-houses, such as those at Crag, near Hepple, 937998, at Hole, near Bellingham, 867847, at Branshaw, near Otterburn, 880997, and at High Shaw, 935982, had stone, barrel-vaulted roofs to their ground-floor. In all bastles there had to be some form of internal access between the ground floor and that above so that the man who secured the stock-door was not left in the dark discomfort of an unheated room. Narrow openings in the stone vault, the timbered floor, or even a very narrow stair within the wall thickness seem to have been the usual solution.

Most bastles were probably originally roofed with heather thatch, but in subsequent more peaceful times this was replaced by slate. Although some are now roofless and ruinous, many have survived, and, though substantially altered to suit modern circumstances, still illustrate their original purpose. Hole Bastle, by the minor road from Bellingham to West Woodburn, close to but separate from the present farmhouse, shows a massive, window-less north wall to the passing motorist, but its south side is almost identical to Gatehouse north bastle. Raw bastle, 942980, above the Grasslees Burn, rather narrower than most, had its upper floor partially rebuilt in the nineteenth century, and forms part of a compact farm group, while at Akeld, 957296, two miles west of Wooler is the same two-storeyed structure mentioned in a Border survey of 1541 as the 'Lytle fortlett or castle house without a barmekyn'. An earlier mention, 1522, in a letter written by Lord Dacre to Cardinal Wolsey, refers to the stationing of ten men there under the command of John Wallis for the defence of the Border, yet from the track which passes its eastern side it resembles nothing more than a large stone barn.

At Housesteads Roman fort, and frequently mistaken for part of the fort, some ground-floor masonry survives of a bastle-house built against the fort's southern wall. Its thick walls are naturally built of Roman masonry, and in the seventeenth century Housesteads bastle was the probable dwelling of one Hugh Nixon, known as a stealer of cattle and a receiver of stolen goods. The Northumbrian historian, Hodgson, records that 'Housesteads was once celebrated as the seat of a daring clan of thieves of the name of Armstrong'. Camden, in 1599, wrote that the area was 'infamous for thieving and robbing', and admitted that he dared not make a close study of the Wall 'for the rank robbers thereabouts'.

Bastle-houses were appearing on the scene certainly by about 1540, a few probably earlier, and were not being superceded much before the Restoration in 1660. They occurred most commonly in Redesdale, North Tynedale and Coquetdale, although some have been identified as far south as Allendale. Historians now suggest that the conditions of Border unrest are not in themselves a sufficient explanation for their building. Rather is it a combination of factors: scattered settlement, nearness to a frontier, availability of good building stone, allied to historical and political changes which, in Border country, created a transitional period when feudal power was decaying but had not yet been replaced by state power. Thus, ordinary farmers had the need for defensible structures and the resources with which to build them.

Tower-houses are one of the distinctive architectural features of Border country, on both Scottish and English sides, and mark a definite response to physical, historic and social conditions which are unique in Britain. In Northumberland (and Cumberland) they are peles. In their earliest defensive form these were of timber, built within a barmkin, or timber-fenced corral, but by the fourteenth century the towers were built of stone. By then the king had permitted, without special licence to crenellate, small defensive fortifications near the Scottish Border. Tower-houses continued to be built even in the late sixteenth century, but most of those which survive are of fourteenth- and fifteenth-century date.

Each pele was a fortified house, complete in itself and not associated with other defensible or military structures, other than a barmkin, none of which now remain. Stone walls were three or four feet thick, and peles were usually of three storeys above a stone-vaulted ground floor which served as a store-room, or even as a refuge for livestock. Pennant and Gilpin both suggested that horses or even cattle could be housed on this ground floor, but the restricted space within the thick walls would have been very limited.

Hodgson's description of the Vicar's Pele at the top of the large green at Elsdon, gives a picture of the interior of this famous pele two centuries ago:

> . . . the first floor (ie ground floor) consisted of a dark vault spanned by one arch, in which in former times the Rector's cattle were housed by night; a circular stone staircase still leads to the upper rooms on the first of which was a kitchen and servants' apartments, flagged with stone; and above these another room, fitted up as a lodging room and study, the bed being in a large recess, with closets on each side, one of which serves as a wardrobe, and the other for more general purposes.
>
> Formerly there were two low rooms above, each containing four chambers . . . Mr Singleton, Rector from 1812, has converted the dark damp vault into a comfortable drawing-room 27ft by 15ft, beside a recess 7ft deep, cut through the wall to the window. The old kitchen and room which was Mr Mitford's parlour (rector 1674–1715) are two bedrooms; and the floor above is occupied by a bedroom, dressing-room and library. To the old building Mr Singleton has added a vestibule and kitchen, and dining-room 26ft by 14ft, and bedrooms above these: besides a back kitchen, pantry and other offices.

All of which underlines the fact that old buildings change as successive occupants adapt them to their own needs and the dictates of changing fashions. But the basic rectangular plan of the pele survives. Some later examples had a timbered vault, still with direct access to the first floor by spiral staircase. Normal access to the first floor was by external ladder or stone staircase, where a heavy oak door would have the extra protection of a hinged iron grill. This first floor would have the main living-room or hall, with a fireplace and small square windows. The chamber, or private room above, would also probably have a fireplace, and there may have been small attic rooms above this. The top of the tower would have a steeply-pitched, gabled roof, slate or shingle-covered, or sometimes flat and lead-covered. Between it and the battlements, usually corbelled out from the wall face, was a walkway and sometimes a small lookout tower was raised at one corner.

Although outside dimensions of peles were 40-45ft (12-14m) by about 30ft (9m), wall-thickness reduced the available floor-area within to less than 30ft by 20ft (9 by 6m). Nevertheless, peles were sophisticated, fortified homes offering effective though passive defence against lightly-armed raiders. They were not intended to withstand prolonged siege by an army. That so many have survived, albeit altered or extended, is a tribute to the success of their sturdy structure in fulfilling the function for which they were designed.

At Corbridge the Vicar's Pele stands in a corner of the churchyard adjoining the Market Place. Dating from about 1300 it is particularly well-built, of Roman masonry from Corstopitum. Three storeys high, with an embattled parapet carried round the corners on projecting corbels, it has a ground floor entrance leading to a vaulted basement which now houses a Tourist Information Office. A stairway within the wall thickness mounts to the first-floor living-room, now used as an Exhibition Centre. The three small windows, a window seat and fireplace help to preserve a picture of relatively comfortable conditions enjoyed by the vicars of Corbridge's large parish who lived in the pele until 1660. Corbridge has another, smaller pele at the eastern end of Main Street dating from about 1600, and having a late seventeenth-century house built on to it.

Very few peles survive within the National Park area. That at Biddlestone, 958083, mentioned in the surveys of 1415 and 1541, forms the ground floor of a modern Roman Catholic chapel, while at Kirknewton church north-west of Wooler, the chancel and south transept may be the survivors of a tower which was mentioned at Kirknewton in both 1415 and 1541, and was known to exist in 1584, a few years after the village had suffered a particularly severe raid by 2,000 horsemen who seized 400 cattle and horses, and took 200 prisoners.

The Vicar's Pele at Alnham, 990110, at the foot of the eastern slopes of the Cheviots, had become ruinous by 1663, and remained so until early last century, when it was restored, the windows re-fashioned, and parapets added to the roof. A new wing was also added, and, during the 1950s and 1960s, the building was used as a Youth Hostel. It has now reverted into private ownership. Thropton Tower, at the western end of the Coquetdale village west of Rothbury, has also been modernised and is still occupied, but does retain original first-floor windows, together with one in the west gable which would have illuminated an attic room.

Nearby, Hepple Tower, almost hidden by trees, seems far more ruinous now than when I first remember it many years ago, while at Great Tosson, on the south side of the Coquet, the remains of the fifteenth century tower of the Ogle family has lost the outer masonry of its walls, leaving the rubble core of pale sandstone as hard as concrete. A reminder that insecurity during Tudor times extended to the southern parts of the county is exemplified at Ninebanks, 782532, a hamlet above the River West Allen. A tower, now incorporated into a farm building, was

*The Vicar's Pele (c1300) at Corbridge*

probably part of a large pele, originally of four storeys, but the adjoining road has been raised so much that it is level with a basement ventilation slit. Also in Allendale, though in the densely-wooded lower part of the valley, Staward Pele, 799607, eight miles west of Hexham, occupies an almost impregnable site, high on a rocky spur with the River Allen on one side and the Harsingdale burn on the other. Two gaunt walls remain of this fourteenth-century pele, and traces of the barmkin can be identified.

It seems probable that for military purposes Staward was succeeded by Thomas Lucy's new castle at Langley, 835625, a few miles to the north-east, and situated in a more strategic position to command the South Tyne valley. This large, impressive tower-house, built about 1350, and a property of the Percy earls of Northumberland and their descendants for over five centuries, was itself ruinous in 1541, but was sympathetically restored in the 1880s by the Northumberland historian, Cadwallader Bates. Its basic rectangular plan, 80 by 24ft (24 by 7m), is partially hidden and dominated by four huge corner towers 66ft (20m) high. It is now used as an hotel offering excellent facilities for conferences and social functions.

Fighting, feuding and raiding went on into the 1590s between the Scots and English, most of it small-scale but occasionally erupting into more official battles. Then suddenly, after the turn of the century, the Tudor dynasty ended with the death of Elizabeth I. James VI of Scotland assumed the English throne, the crowns of England and Scotland were united in 1603, the age of peace began, and sheep could once again graze peacefully the broad Border uplands.

The effect on the landscape was initially less dramatic than that on the local architecture. The needs of defence were past; confidence in the future promoted a greater desire for comfort in the home. Although it is well to the east of our area, nowhere in the county is this transition shown so splendidly as at Belsay, by the A696. Belsay Castle is a superb, L-shaped tower-house built about 1370 with impressive corner-turrets and machiolated battlements. Within a dozen years of the Union of the Crowns an elegant, early Jacobean-style country house had been added to it, with large mullioned windows looking southwards over calm parkland. Above the renaissance doorway an inscription reads, 'Thomas Middleton and Dorothy his wife builded this house 1614'. They felt safe enough to do so. Belsay Castle and the early nineteenth-century Hall a mile away are now in the care of English Heritage.

Halton Tower, above Corbridge, also had a graceful seventeenth-century house added to the older pele, and is now occupied privately. Bellister Castle, opposite Haltwhistle, now National Trust property though not open to the public, has a castellated farmhouse of 1669 added on to a ruined pele, while two miles to the south-west, Featherstone

*Featherstone Castle, by the South Tyne. Though mainly an early nineteenth-century piece of Romantic Gothic, its nucleus is a large tower-house of c1330*

Castle, 674610, by the South Tyne, though mainly an early nineteenth-century piece of Romantic Gothic, has as its nucleus a large tower-house of c1330.

Perhaps the building which best illustrates the transition from medieval stronghold to seventeenth- and eighteenth-century farmhouse is Williemoteswick, shown on the map as Williemontswick, 770635, above the riverside haughs of the South Tyne opposite Bardon Mill and at the end of a 'No Through Road'. Very little is known about this former home of the Ridleys, although it was described in 1541 as 'a good tower and stone house adjoining thereto, of the inheritance of Nicholas Ridley, and kept in good reparations'. The 1415 list makes no reference to it. Like many Northumbrian farms of the eighteenth or early nineteenth centuries it is in effect a self-contained hamlet, based on an inner courtyard, the entrance to which, in this case, is through a well-preserved medieval gatehouse. The west range opposite contains, within more recent buildings, two unusual narrow towers, probably the gables of an earlier structure.

The course of Northumbrian history, particularly on the fringes of the uplands, is repeatedly expressed in the sequence of buildings on the same site; medieval pele or stronghold followed first by Jacobean mansion and then by the classical house and its park associated with subsequent wealth

*The well-preserved medieval gatehouse entrance to Williemoteswick*

and fashion of the eighteenth century. Chipchase Castle, 883757 in the North Tyne valley exemplifies this perfectly. Seen from the north-west, or from the minor road between Wark and Chollerton on the east side of the valley, it appears a typical pele of the mid-fourteenth century, and as such was the accepted residence of the Keeper of Tynedale, responsible not only for protecting the local population against Scots raids from the north, but for keeping them in order themselves. In 1621, Cuthbert Heron added a handsome new mansion to the south-east side of the tower, in which false windows were inserted to improve the symmetry. The great expanses of windows in the Jacobean mansion were themselves enlarged in 1784, and even the original tower received three tiers of regular windows.

A few miles down-river, but on the west bank, Haughton Castle, initially a modest fortified house, was enlarged to a castle in 1373, on a rather similar plan to that at Langley, but with the unusual feature of having five tall arches erected on both north and south sides, to support the newly added storey. These were later filled in. By 1541 the castle was described as being in great decay. In the late eighteenth century William Smith restored Haughton, and Salvin added a new west wing in 1876. When the park was created in 1816 Haughton village was destroyed, the people being moved to, and re-housed in, the new village of Humshaugh a mile to the south. The meagre ruins of a medieval chapel survive, rather forlornly, in Haughton's wooded park. A public footpath which gave access to the long-vanished ferry to Barrasford across the river, now affords a good view of Haughton Castle, seen preferably in the sunlight of a summer evening.

The more peaceful conditions which followed the Union of the Crowns in 1603 encouraged landowners and lesser gentry to build more comfortable houses but made little or no difference to the living standards of the peasant population. In the National Park area no examples of small vernacular buildings of the seventeenth century survive, and relatively few of the first half of the eighteenth century. Indeed, when William Cobbett visited Northumberland in 1832, staying at Alnwick, Morpeth and Hexham, he was able to describe the farmhouses as 'big enough and fine enough for a gentleman to live in', adding that, associated with them were bothies or sheds for unmarried labourers, and single-storey barracks of stone for the married. These latter would be the terraces of cottages which today are still a characteristic feature of upland Northumberland. When they were built, probably in the early years of last century, they had floors of beaten earth, walls of rubble sandstone, small square windows which, if they opened at all, would have had the horizontal sliding sash so common in cottages of the Yorkshire Pennines almost a century earlier, two-part doors of the 'stable' type, and roofs of heather thatch. Unlike the better miners' cottages being built at the same time, labourers' cottages in the upland areas probably had no bedrooms in the roof space. Now, many are holiday cottages or second homes, their windows modernised, their roofs of slate or pantile, space for one or two small bedrooms in the roof lit by inserted dormer windows, and with a modern kitchen added to the rear of the building.

Typically, in Redesdale, North Tynedale, and along the eastern and southern foothills of the Cheviots, where hamlets or farm-towns are the characteristic form of settlement, they are usually centred on a four-square, mid- or late-eighteenth-century farmhouse. These sturdy houses, usually of grey-brown sandstone, slate-roofed with Georgian windows, too frequently spoiled by having lost their glazing bars in favour of large Victorian panes, are invariably two-storey, but with few concessions to ostentation. Dignified symmetry resulted from the central door flanked by windows illuminating the single rooms on each side, with three matching windows above. Roofs almost always ended with gables and flat copings, the base stones of which were usually kept simple, but occasionally show decorative carving as a particular feature. Shillmoor, 886076, in the Coquet valley above Alwinton, illustrates perfectly the eighteenth-century resettlement farmstead and associated buildings in an area probably last colonised under the monasteries in medieval times.

In the Cheviot foothills, south of Wooler, the small village of Ilderton, 017218, is virtually a single farm, its various buildings still showing in their massive structure more than an echo of the former needs of defence, and it is a fine example of the eighteenth- and nineteenth-century rebuilding of a self-contained medieval farm settlement. Kilham, in the Bowmont valley, and Kirknewton, have long terraces of single-storey cottages, while at Akeld similar cottages, dated late eighteenth century, form two sides of a courtyard of farm buildings. Farther south Chollerton, 933721, in the North Tyne valley, is a typical 'farm-town' whose late-Georgian farmhouse looks across to a long terrace of two-storey labourers' cottages, and the extensive range of agricultural buildings include stables, byres, the sail-less remains of a stone-built tower windmill, and the surviving brick chimney of a steam-engine house which, in mid-Victorian times, provided power for the threshing machines.

Within a year of the Union of Crowns (1603), James I initiated a Border Survey. In this, referring to Redesdale above Elsdon, it was reported that 'certain high lands called summer grounds are used as summer and shieling grounds by the whole inhabitants of the Manor, wherein each man knoweth his shieling stead; and they shield together by Surnames; not keeping Cattle according to the proportion of the rent, but eating all in Common without stint or number'. Five years earlier, Queen Elizabeth I's great historian, Camden, gave his description of a shieling. 'Here every way round about in the wasts as they tearme them, you may see as it were the ancient Nomades, a martiall kind of men, who from the moneth of April unto August, lye out scattering and summering (as they tearme it) with their cattell in little cottages here and there which they call Sheales and Shealings'.

This transhumance system of pastoral farming showed the survival of Celtic influences in the hill country, and was probably unique in sixteenth-century England, although it was much more common in Scotland. A court case in Redesdale in the 1630s referred to men who 'divide up the lowlands by the land itself and they do not divide up the land of their highlands but only the rents and eat the lands in common'. Or rather their stock did, and continue to do so in the unenclosed upland commons above the Allendales and to the south-west of Hexham, where 'stinted grazing' is practised, in which a number of local farmers have the right to graze a specific number of cattle and sheep on the commons.

In the sixteenth century farmers in Redesdale had their summerings on the uplands west of the Rede, after the bere (barley) was sown; Tynedale's shielings were to the south of the Coquet, while Newminster Abbey's flocks and herds, before the Dissolution, grazed the high lands of Kidlandlee. Most of the shielings continued in use well into the sixteenth century, and, in some remote places, until the wide-ranging farming improvements of the eighteenth century. The repeated use of 'shiels' as

*Farm labourers' housing forming two sides of a courtyard at Akeld, near Wooler*

suffix in a place-name testifies to the extent of this system of summer pasturing, while the 'hope' suffix, meaning a sheltered valley for grazing, is additional evidence. Hill country held in common, and used as grazing areas often some considerable distance from a home settlement, was – and still is – called 'outbye'. Arable land for cultivation close to a settlement was, and is, the 'inbye', and after harvest time its stubble would provide winter grazing for any stock mainly sheep, kept then.

After the Union of Crowns, although more peaceful farming conditions prevailed, an ancient system of partible inheritance prevented any real progress. In this, when a man died his lands were shared equally among his sons. As a result, not only were the individual holdings too small to be viable units, but they had to support an increased population. In addition, the shared nature of the common grazings discouraged possible improvements to them. Changes came about, but only slowly, and these were largely through the process of Enclosure.

Enclosure was not a new thing. After the Dissolution of the Monasteries in the late 1530s land at Clennell and Biddlestone in upper Coquetdale formerly owned by Newminster Abbey had been turned into a deer park with a wall round it. Even before the end of that century some landowners were dividing up common fields to form smaller units enclosed by hedges and ditches. Large areas of arable land in open field

*Chollerton, near Hexham, a typical 'farm-town', showing farm labourers' housing on the left, barns, stables, the tower of a windmill, an engine-house chimney, and part of the late Georgian farmhouse on the right*

systems was being turned over to pasture for sheep-grazing and the Cheviots, peaceable once more, became vast sheep-walks; although it was not until the middle of last century that boundaries of ownership were delineated by walls and fences.

Until 1603 landowners depended on their tenants for military services in return for low, fixed rents and the right to sub-let. This system of customary tenure was gradually replaced during the seventeenth century by one of leasehold, and it was this which gave landlords the chance to enclose moorland, wastes and hill pastures. However, this outbye land being held in common, it was necessary for landowners to obtain Enclosure Awards through Act of Parliament. These awards allowed for areas of common land to be enclosed, and compensated commoners with parcels of land in exchange for the loss of their grazing rights. Enclosure Awards also granted quarries for parish use, and set out the lines of new roads, bridleways and footpaths, and it is along many of these that we drive, ride and walk today.

Few roads in the area give such a splendid picture of the landscapes created by the mid-eighteenth century 'improving landowners' as the Corn Road (see Chapter 6), particularly in its section between the A68 and Forestburn Gate, 066963, beyond which it runs along the National Park boundary towards Rothbury. Had Pennant travelled this way he would have given a vastly different description. In the first half of the century Sir William Loraine of Kirkharle is said to have planted 24,000 forest trees, 488,000 quicks (hawthorns) and 580 fruit trees in developing his inherited estates, and it was to him that the sixteen-year old Lancelot Brown was apprenticed in 1732 to learn about the nascent art of landscape gardening. His early training here in central Northumberland must surely have exerted a strong influence which stayed with him through a long life, and it is these same civilised, ordered parklands that present such a pleasant surprise to travellers from the south who expect to find harsh and dour landscapes.

Loraine's neighbour, Sir Walter Calverly Blackett followed suit, and transformed 'many square miles of Northumberland by road-making, building and planting between 1730 and 1770' on his huge Wallington estates. Brown may have contributed in small scale by advising on the

Rothley lakes, and it was the eminent architect, James Paine, who designed the elegant, three-arched stone bridge spanning the River Wansbeck on the southern approach to Wallington in 1760, conforming with the classical lines of planned landscapes. About the same time Cambo village was laid out in the charming formality enjoyed by present-day visitors, and now includes a full range of village and estate buildings spanning the past two centuries. Indeed, the post office occupies part of an 1818 reconstruction of a former pele tower.

In North Tynedale the Swinburnes, from their home at Swinburne Castle, itself an elegant late eighteenth century rebuilding of an older house, initiated large-scale enclosures of the open fields below the house and on the moorlands above, on both sides of Dere Street. These 'improving' processes were a continuing factor in landscape change well into the nineteenth century.

When Arthur Young travelled through Northumberland in the 1770s he reported that, of the county's 1¼ million acres (500,000 ha), 'there were at least 600,000 acres waste and great tracts were covered in broom and gorse'. Although this could not have been any more than a reasoned estimate it is, nevertheless, a fair indication of the extent of unenclosed, unused land. Within three generations the picture had changed to such an extent that Northumberland was the leading agricultural county in England. Enclosure Awards were made for individual parishes, and it is interesting to pick out a few, with their dates, to see how and when the landscapes throughout the area gained the pattern we see today.

Elsdon Common, north of the village, was the subject of one of the earliest Enclosure Awards, 1729, but the general period of enclosure there and in Tynedale coincided with the decades of general agricultural prosperity, 1770–1850. Enclosures of those years had effects on the landscape just as dramatic as afforestation of the past fifty years. Fields of various sizes were separated by earthen banks planted with quickset hedges, usually hawthorn, creating barriers impenetrable to stock, but soon found favour with many species of birds. Variety of shrub species in a short 30yd (27m) length of hedge is a guide to its age, and few Northumbrian hedges are more than two centuries old, many of them younger than that, with only one or two shrub species. When the naturalist, Thomas Pennant returned southwards from his Scottish trip in the 1770s he noted that the country south of Cornhill (ie Glendale, north of Wooler) was 'open, destitute of trees and almost of hedges'.

Drive today along that north-eastern edge of the Cheviots, by the A697 through Wooler, and you see the ordered landscapes of Glendale. On the opposite side of the road to Coupland with its late pele-tower are the woods and shelter-belts and neat hedged fields of Ewart Park. A few

(above right) *Housey Crag, Harthope Valley;* (right) *Elsdon Pele Tower*

years after Pennant's visit, Horace Paul, who became a Count of the Holy Roman Empire, returned from the British Embassy in Paris to his Northumberland estate in 1787, rebuilt the old house and set about creating a model estate in the precise geometry of the eighteenth century. Although some was destroyed with the building of an airfield, 1939–45, sufficient remains to present a picture of typical formality.

Nearby, the brothers George and Matthew Culley, who came from south Durham and were greatly influenced by the famous stock-breeder Robert Bakewell of Leicester, settled in Glendale, initially at Coupland and later at Fowberry Tower three miles east of Wooler. By 1800 they tenanted six large farms, paying a rental of £4,000–£5,000 a year. Soon after they became landlords they were making almost £10,000 a year profit, ditching, draining, embanking and hedging their land, turning huge areas of broom-covered waste into some of the best land in the county. They soon persuaded local Cheviot sheep-breeders to try a Leicester cross, and by the mid-nineteenth century the Border Leicester, as it became called, was being extensively used for crossing with other breeds, but not with the Cheviots themselves.

George Culley collaborated with his neighbour John Bailey to produce the *General View of the Agriculture of the County of Northumberland*, first published in 1794. In it was this comment about enclosures:

> The parts of the county capable of cultivation are in general well inclosed by high hedges; the only exception is a small part of the Vales of Breamish, Till and Glen, but even here the advantage of having well-fenced fields is so well understood, and so much desired by the tenants, that we hope, in eight or ten years, the whole of this valuable district will be inclosed by fences. The size of the inclosure varies with the size of the farms. In some parts from 2 to 6 acres, in the northern parts where the farms are large, the fields are from 20 to 100 acres.

Culley also gives the specifications for the construction of the stone walls or dykes commonly used as field boundaries in the hill areas of Cheviot, Redesdale and above both of the Tyne valleys: '2½ feet at the bottom, 15 or 16 inches at the top, 4-4½ feet high, with a row of through stones, 9 or 10 in a 7-yard rood'. Variation occurred from one area to another, usually according to the availability of walling stone. Where Fell Sandstone prevailed, walls tended to be higher and thicker than on the Cheviots, where good walling stone is relatively scarce; yet even there walls are double-skinned, the two parts leaning slightly together and the space between them packed with small stones, *filler* or *chatter*. Today, where new walls are necessary or repairs to existing ones are needed, most farmers are capable of doing the job themselves in the traditional way.

*Elsdon Village Green*

However, the National Park Authority, the Forestry Commission and the County Council do employ a few professional wallers; a job suited only to those rugged characters who like hard work and solitude, and can show an enviable degree of patience and skill. One yard of drystone wall requires about 1¾ tons (1,780kg) of stone, and can cost at least £10. One farm in North Tynedale, typical of many, has about 10 miles (16km) of walls, representing over 30,000 tons of stone to be quarried, carted and built into walls. When that land was enclosed in the 1870s, the contract rate of pay was 7 shillings (35p) a rudd (7yd: 6.4m), and one man would build this amount of wall in a 14-hour working day.

Thus do we gain an impression of the sheer slog of building the walls that line the lonely uplands from the Scottish Border to the north-eastern slopes of Cross Fell. Mention has been made of one of the earliest Enclosure Awards, at Elsdon in 1729. The second half of the eighteenth century saw the rate of enclosure accelerate. During the three preceding centuries the Hexhamshire Commons had gradually been whittled away at their periphery, through Crown grants and illegal enclosures, and the soil and mineral rights belonged, as usual, to the lord of the manor. Various land holdings in and around Hexham included rights of grazing on the remaining 8,000 acres (3.200ha) of the East and West Commons. An Enclosure Award of 1753 enacted that 'the Commons should be set out, allotted and divided by 1 May 1756'. The Award also gave the lord of the manor, Sir William Blackett, one-sixteenth part of this common adjoining his estate at Yarridge (near Hexham Racecourse) as compensation for his ownership of the soil. As a result the landscape pattern over twelve square miles, west of Hexham and south of the Tyne to opposite Newbrough, was radically changed in the space of three years. Further Enclosure Awards on the Hexham and Allendale Commons in 1800, covering about 42,000 acres (16,800ha), embracing almost all of the uplands between the Devil's Water and the West Allen, southwards to the Durham border, completed the transformation.

These enclosures have given us the straight roads now known as the B6305 running westwards from Hexham to Lowgate, south-west to East and West Nubbock, westwards to Stublick and eastwards past the racecourse. These, like many enclosure roads, are characterised by their width between the walls or hedges bordering each side, usually at least 30ft (9m), sometimes more, with wide grass verges. On both sides of the road from Lowgate to Stublick the enclosed fields create a regular pattern of squares and rectangles, with small copses, coverts and shelter-belts.

(pp86-7) *The plantations and shelter-belts of a well-farmed countryside, looking north across the South Tyne valley, from Moralees Wood above Allen Banks. The Whin Sill skyline is beyond*

Not all enclosure roads continued in use, and Cushat Lane, running north from Lowgate, 905640, is a good example of a disused road, still 30ft (9m) wide, with coarse tussocky grass between its bordering fences, whose line is broken by straggling hawthorns and a few hedgerow trees. The lane, and the landscape through which it passes, dates from the 1753 enclosure of Hexham East Common. Unlike the turnpike roads with which many enclosure roads are contemporary, there was no obligation for milestones to be positioned, although some were added later by highway authorities.

The real surge of enclosure activity got under way after Young's visit, with enclosure at Corbridge and Stagshaw Bank in 1776, Melkridge, near Haltwhistle, 1783, Langley in 1792, and Grindon in 1796. The Napoleonic Wars, with their resultant demands for an increase in home-grown crops, tended to accelerate enclosure of marginal land on the uplands. Soon after the turn of the century Thirlwall Common and Doddington Moor were enclosed, while between 1805 and 1809 thousands of acres of moorland at Elsdon, Tosson, Hepple, Corsenside, Simonburn and Tarretburn, although brought under control by enclosure walls and hedges, did not necessarily suffer a change of land use, but still remained pasture, albeit improved by burning or ploughing,

*Grindon Hill, by the Stanegate. A characteristic late-eighteenth-century farmhouse within its sheltering trees*

*Hotbank Farm, built in the late-eighteenth century, using Roman masonry*

draining and liming, and reseeding with grass. 6,000 acres (2,400ha) of Rothbury Forest were enclosed in 1831, about 7,500 acres (3,000ha) of the Hareshaw moors above Bellingham in 1845, and over 3,000 acres (1,200ha) of Plenmeller Commons near Haltwhistle at the same time. One of the last great moorland enclosures in Northumberland involved the cold, sombre Pennine wilderness of Knarsdale Common, above the South Tyne valley, where 12,000 acres (4,800ha) of cotton-grass wastes were enclosed in 1859. Here, as on the other moors, miles of stone walls stitch the bare uplands.

Contrasting with such lonely, little-visited areas are more intimate ones above Wooler. The common lands between Humbleton and Akeld were enclosed in 1867, and Wooler Common, between the town and Humbleton, was enclosed two years later, when nine freeholders were allotted under one acre of land each as compensation for losing their pasture rights on the common. Some prehistoric cairns in this area and elsewhere on the Cheviots were dismantled at this time to provide stone for the new boundary walls, and it is said that the remains of the Bronze Age 'Tom Tallon's Grave', 933280, on the hills south-west of Akeld provided enough stone to build a wall 1,000yd long, 5ft high and over 2ft thick (914 x 1.5 x .6m).

Enclosures, both of the former open fields (where these existed) of villages, and subsequently of the upland wastes, in addition to creating the needs for new roads, also encouraged the building of farmsteads more convenient to the newly-enclosed lands. This, together with the peaceful and stabilised conditions which followed the Act of Union of 1707, largely explains why there are so few farmhouses and associated buildings earlier than the eighteenth century in rural Northumberland. Indeed, few farms in the upland area date from before 1750, and many are of early nineteenth-century date. On the Stanegate, and at the south-eastern corner of the National Park, 830681, the farmhouse and buildings of Grindon Hill are a typical product of these new conditions, perhaps architecturally better than most.

It may be the greater availability of good stone, either from quarries or from the Roman Wall, that has resulted in the farms and some village houses in this area, in the North Tyne valley, in Allendale, and on the edges of the Simonside Hills, being superior to those in Cheviot country, where, on the whole, local architecture is disappointing. Visually, farm buildings in the Allendales are more exciting than elsewhere in the Northumbrian uplands, and they are more closely related culturally to their Pennine counterparts farther south.

Apart from Hexhamshire with almost 5,000 acres (2,000ha) and Allendale, 18,000 acres (7,200ha), very few parts of the Northumbrian uplands survive as common land. Sixty acres (24ha) of Stagshaw Common near Portgate continue to be grazed by tenants of local farms, and there are a few very small village greens. Within the National Park area, only the 20 acres (8ha) of Sharperton Haughs, east of Harbottle, are a significant survival, and the Cheviots are probably a unique range of hills in possessing no common land at all.

# 5

# INDUSTRIAL ARCHAEOLOGY

Although pastoral farming has always been the main occupation in the Northumbrian uplands other industries have left their scars, particularly the extractive processes of stone-quarrying, iron-working, lead-mining and, to a lesser extent, coal-mining. Within the National Park area mineral extraction has never occurred on a large scale, and at present only one quarry is operating commercially, at Biddlestone, near Alwinton, its hard rock being used for roadstone. The conspicuously red felsite obtained from Harden Quarry not only creates the colour of many local road surfaces but it had the distinction of being used to provide the attractive red 'carpet' along the Mall in London.

Walltown Quarry near Greenhead, which was opened in 1871 and closed around 1950, produced whinstone, not only as chippings for agglomerate and road surfaces, but also as hand-cut paving setts or cobble stones used in market squares. Although whinstone was almost too hard to be a building stone a few buildings by the road at Walltown were constructed from large blocks of this dour material.

Travellers using the A696 will notice the large spoil heaps on the crest of Hunterlee Hill three miles south-east of Otterburn. Blaxter's Quarry was first worked early last century, yielding greyish sandstone easily quarried and cut, so that it was relatively quick and cheap to produce. Raylees farmhouse, by the Elsdon turning, is thought to be the first local building constructed of this stone, in 1821, whose quality took it much farther afield, particularly to Ireland and Scotland, where it was used extensively in Princes Street, Edinburgh, as well as for restoration work on the famous Abbey at Iona. Blaxter's Quarry reached the end of its profitable working life of over 150 years, in 1984, when it was finally closed.

Many other long-abandoned quarries mark small sites where good-quality sandstones were obtained for use in local buildings. Among these is that at Fourstones, north-west of Hexham, from which came the stone used by John Dobson for his monumental Central Station at Newcastle. Prudham freestone, as the material is called, is now working again, after a period of inactivity. Limestone is also quarried near Fourstones.

## Lime

During his 1770 tour through the north of England Arthur Young found it 'very melancholy to ride through such vastly extensive tracks of uncultivated good land, as are found in every part of this county'. But a start had been made on enclosing land on the moor edge. After walling, enclosed land was burned to remove rough heather, sedge and occasionally bracken. Then it was drained, after which lime was added to sweeten the soil in the hope of producing good pasture.

Huge amounts of lime were needed. Limestone was readily available over much of the area but in order to convert this into usable lime, kilns were necessary. Many of these survive, some are impressive enough to give an idea of their construction and operation. They are easily identified by their dark, cave-like mouths in the front of turret-like structures, sometimes seen from a road, but more frequently hidden away near convenient limestone outcrops. Records show that lime-burning as a local industry seems to have spanned the century from 1780–1880, most of it concentrated in the period 1810–30.

Most limekilns produced lime for use on the farm or estate where they were built, any surplus probably being sold to neighbouring farms. Among the larger kilns which worked on a commercial basis were the splendid pair at Crindledykes, 781670, by the minor road between Chesterholm and the B6318, which are a Grade 2 listed building. These have a circular plan, are stone-built and have a turf roof. The two large openings towards the road have stepped, pointed arches of shell-shaped section, and there is another opening at the rear. Similar kilns occur by the Pennine Way, north of Hotbank Crags, which, like other examples, show the characteristic choice of site, built into a hillside near a source of limestone, and preferably handy to a source of coal.

*Lime kilns at Crindledykes, above Bardon Mill*

In use, quarried stone broken into small pieces was loaded into the bowl-shaped firing chamber with alternating layers of coal, to give a sandwiched mixture of four parts of lime to one part of coal. This was burned, emitting clouds of smoke, and as the mixture burned and settled, further charges of limestone and fuel would be added, so that even a small 'field' kiln might burn continuously for two or three days, a commercial kiln for a week or more. The resultant mixture of lime and ash was raked out from the hearth at the bottom of the bowl and at the back of the kiln's mouth. Even a few days' firing could produce 300 horse-loads of lime, each of 2 cwt (130kg), either for a farmer's own use or for selling at, perhaps 4d a load (2p). Four loads made a cartful, and ten carts could carry sufficient lime for an acre of land. Limekilns were costly to build and the fuel, transport and wages associated with them usually cancelled out any profit. Although most of the lime produced was used as a soil-sweetener, some provided the basis for lime mortar used in the building of farmhouses, barns and cottages which were being constructed at that time. Now, the kilns are silent and derelict, convenient dumps for a variety of rubbish, sad memorials to a vanished rural industry.

## Coal

Coal from outcrops on or near the surface has been worked in many places over the area since medieval times, but until early last century pits were small and localised in their influence. An interesting reference to coal working in Redesdale comes from the Elsdon Parish Register which records the burial on 17 July 1691 of a relative of William Ward, 'colyer at Rattenraw'. By the middle of the eighteenth century coal was obtained from numerous small pits in Redesdale and its tributary valleys, and most working was by bell pits or short adits. A bell pit was a single shaft sunk the few feet necessary to reach a workable seam – in the case of Redesdale and the North Tyne valleys this was probably the Plashetts Coal, a 4-6ft (1.2-1.8m) seam within the Scremerston Coal Group – and from the foot of the shaft the miners worked radially outwards to the limits of a safe distance, probably not more than a few yards. Then another shaft would be sunk along the seam, worked to safe limits as before, and so on. Much of the coal was splint coal, mixed with quantities of shale, and suitable only for fuelling limekilns or adding to the peat used on domestic fires. Larger workings at Brownrigg and Elsdon, and later Bellshiel, yielded coal of a quality to justify continued production for local use. Bellshiel closed in 1935, but Elsdon survived as a privately-owned colliery until 1972. Only the grass-covered spoil-heaps and the silted-up bell-pits surrounded by their raised discs of waste, remain as visual reminders of the scale and appearance of rural coal-mining in Redesdale.

The wide valley of the North Tyne above Falstone was the unlikely setting for coal-mining on a scale rather larger than in Redesdale, though at no time did it approach in importance or size the scale of operations in the south-east corner of Northumberland. Two large land-owning families played an important part in its development. The Percys held extensive estates on the north side of the North Tyne based on their impressive shooting-lodge, Kielder Castle, built in 1775. South of the river much of the land belonged to the Swinburnes of Capheaton, who had a more modest shooting-lodge at Mounces. They had also built a number of neat stone bridges spanning various tributary burns. Both estates used local coal to heat their estate buildings, but the Swinburnes were exploiting their Lewisburn drift mine commercially by the early 1840s. Packhorses carried loads of coal up the old track by the Akenshaw Burn, westwards over the Larriston Fells into Liddesdale.

On the Border line at Bloodybush Edge, on the edge of Kielder Forest, 572910, a large stone pillar commemorates the improvement of this track, and its faded inscription is shown overleaf.

A few years later, in 1851, two gamekeepers on the Percy estates were allowed to re-open a small drift mine at Plashetts with the stipulation that they provided coal for Kielder Castle. This mine, and the exposure of associated coal seams nearby, indicated there were good quantities of usable coal, sufficient to justify commercial exploitation provided the local transport system could be improved to allow sale in the Scottish Border towns and even on Tyneside.

The Newcastle-Hexham-Carlisle railway line had been established in 1839, and astute investors were considering the potential of the mineral resources of the North Tyne valley, especially the Plashetts coal, as the lure by which to build a link with Scotland. Indeed, in 1857 the Duke of Northumberland's agent set up a promotional sight-seeing tour for possible investors among influential men on both sides of the Borders. A company, the Border Counties Railway, had already been authorised by Act of Parliament in 1854, and initial construction work had gone quickly enough during the following year, so that by 1856 a line was open from the Border Counties Junction near Hexham, 919654, to Belling Burn, 693882, east of Plashetts.

It had been intended at the outset that the BCR would continue across the Border to join with the planned North British Railway between Carlisle and Hawick. In 1857 the BCR adopted the route between Belling Burn and Riccarton, beyond the Scottish Border, and the line was completed in July 1862, with intermediate stations at Plashetts,

Kielder, Deadwater and Saughtree, and, its most outstanding architectural feature, the Kielder Viaduct. This alone survives from the closure of the line in 1956 and the subsequent creation in the North Tyne valley of the Kielder Reservoir. Its seven skew arches, designed by J. F. Tone, their feet protected by a concrete covering, now stand in six feet of water on the north side of Bakethin Reservoir at the western end of Kielder, and carry a public footpath.

By the time the railway link to Scotland was completed the Plashetts Coal Company was developing its enterprise, opening more drift workings and building a small mining hamlet, appropriately called 'Seldom Seen', up the Belling Burn. However, difficult working conditions and decreasing quality of coal led to the company experiencing financial trouble. In 1884 a new company took over, only to meet similar problems, and five years later a third group of owners, under John Slater, managed to stem the tide and gain some success. The new village of Bank-top was created half a mile downstream from Seldom Seen, with sixty-four houses accommodating a population of between 200 and 300 people, for whom the railway was the only lifeline out of the austere isolation.

The original drift at Plashetts was abandoned, and new ones opened up on the hillside above Plashetts Station, having all the structures

*Kielder Viaduct (c1860) on the Border Counties Railway, now spans the uppermost arm of Bakethin Reservoir*

associated with a working colliery. For over thirty years the isolated community survived, almost prospering for a while as coal continued to be produced. Inevitably most of the people were Methodists; the Duke made land available for them to build a chapel which also served as a school and the community built its own village hall. World War I took its toll of young men, and the 1920s saw the colliery decline, accelerated by the 1926 General Strike. After that, families began to leave Plashetts, and by the middle of the 1930s the end had come. Now, half a century later, only a few foundations lie buried in the grass, Forestry Commission plantations darken the moorland, and Kielder Water covers the rich valley land.

## Iron

In several areas of southern Northumberland the rocks of the Coal Measures contain sufficient quantities of blackband ironstone to justify working, and iron-working in North Tynedale is now known to have been carried out from medieval times near Falstone, while there is evidence from Wark-on-Tyne of an eighteenth-century bloomery. However, its real potential as a suitable iron ore was not realised until 1801, but over thirty years elapsed before it was commercially exploited to any marked extent. Two blast furnaces were started in Redesdale in 1836 and at Hareshaw near Bellingham two years later, to smelt the ironstone which outcropped along both banks of the Hareshaw Burn and over some of the neighbourhood. Plashetts coalfield supplied the necessary fuel. Around 1846 a blast furnace at Chesterwood, near Haydon Bridge in the South Tyne valley, was built to smelt local ores, but did not remain in operation for very long. The most distinctive survival from these rural workings is the ruined engine-house of the Ridsdale ironworks, 909847, on the west side of the A68 south of West Woodburn, often mistaken by travellers as the gaunt keep of a former castle, which it closely resembles. Less conspicuous, but no less significant, is the remains of a masonry dam on the Hareshaw Burn at Bellingham seen by walkers exploring the quiet beauty of this attractive dene.

Usually, nineteenth-century blast furnaces needed three main raw materials: iron ore of adequate grade, a good coking coal, and limestone to act as a flux to remove slag. At Ridsdale and Hareshaw all these were locally available, while Plashetts coal may have supplemented the Hareshaw supply. The ironstone needed roasting, so 'calcining' kilns were built at both works, and the coal used in the final blast furnace operations was initially part-coked in coking ovens.

The air required to raise furnace temperatures to smelting temperatures was pumped in at the base of the furnaces, the air-blast machinery being powered by water-wheels or steam engines. Records indicate that

Hareshaw's three blast furnaces were blown by a seventy horsepower waterwheel and a 120 horsepower steam engine. There were seventy coke ovens and twenty-four roasting kilns, together with a range of stores and service buildings, and ninety company cottages for the workers. Harsh facts of geography ensured that the works were unlikely to prosper, for neither the upper North Tyne nor Redesdale had rail connections with the world beyond. In 1852 the Hareshaw Ironworks were idle, much of the plant derelict, and sixty-eight cottages unoccupied. Ten years later, when the Border Counties line was fully operational, it was too late to save the works, for the discovery of rich iron ores in Cleveland and the mushroom growth of Teesside's iron industry had made their explosive impact on the north-east.

Today only a few grass-covered earthworks mark the site of this short-lived industry. A new factory occupies part of it, and the embankment of the 1862 Border Counties Railway touches the site's southern edge, with a row of six cottages, Bellum Brae, just within it. There were originally ten, with the last but one on the east an estate office for the Duke of Northumberland, whose crest is displayed on a 1901 date panel. On the Hareshaw Burn the 1838 dam stands at only half its original height, while the inhabited terrace of two-storey houses, with gardens backing on to the burn, were company workers' houses with ground-floor accommodation and offices above.

Ridsdale's gaunt engine house formerly housed the double-beam blowing engine which supplied the air to three blast furnaces. Details of the plant arrangement are not known although it seems probable that there were three lines of coke ovens immediately to the south. These, and the calcining kilns, were linked by tramways to ironstone and coal mines and limestone quarries in the neighbourhood, and the course of these tramways can still be traced. After the works closed much of the removeable plant was transferred to the Armstrong works at Elswick, on Tyneside, which also continued to exploit the raw materials of Redesdale and actually constructed more calcining kilns near the head of Broomhope Burn which still survive.

However, the Ridsdale works can claim one famous link, for pig-iron made there went into the mixture for castings and probably for some of the wrought iron used by Robert Stephenson for his unique High Level Bridge of 1846–9 carrying both railway and road across the Tyne at Newcastle.

## Lead mining

No lead is mined in Northumberland today. For almost a century the mines and smelt mills have been silent apart from the reworking of old levels and spoil heaps for fluorite and barite. The industry had peaked around the middle of last century when the price of lead was £32 a ton. In

*Smelt-mill flue and chimney 1845–50, in Allendale*

1896, following the opening of lead mines in Australia, Mexico and the United States, this had fallen to £13 a ton, resulting in the collapse of the British lead industry.

Northumbrian lead mining can be traced to Roman times, for melted lead and fragments of ore at Corstopitum probably came from the Alston mines, which were in Northumberland until the reign of Henry I. In the twelfth century it was complained that lead-miners were destroying woodlands in the lordship of Hexham, especially in the Allendales.

The north Pennine ore-field comprised six distinct areas: Alston Moor, East Allendale, West Allendale, Derwent, Weardale and Teesdale. Only the three of these in Northumberland come within this survey: East Allendale based on Allenheads, West Allendale centred on Coalcleugh, and Derwent centred on Blanchland. From the Durham and Cumbria borders to the valleys of Tyne and Derwent the moorlands are scarred with old workings and spoil heaps, shafts and levels, and the tall chimneys standing like lonely sentinels between the Allendale valleys and above Stublick Syke on the Langley road.

Lead-bearing ore, galena (lead sulphide-PbS) exists as veins, usually near-vertical and extending to great depths in huge cracks penetrating strata in various Pennine limestones. The most productive veins are orientated roughly NE/SW, with local 'flats' occasionally branching off horizontally. Bisecting the ore-field from north to south is the

Burtreeford Fault with a downthrow to the east of 400-500ft (122-152m). This runs along the western side of East Allendale and across Weardale, southwards to Teesdale.

Most veins become poorer in quality the deeper they go, so that there has been no deep mining in the north Pennine ore field, with most mines being less than 100 fathoms (600ft). Earliest workings were on or just below the surface, for once a vein had been located it could easily be followed and worked. To help locate a vein of ore a system known as hushing was used, which involved scouring by water. On the crest of a hill above a suspected vein a turf dam was built, sometimes strengthened with stones, across a moorland watercourse, thus impounding its waters into a small reservoir. When sufficient water was collected the dam was broken and the released water, surging down the hillside, scoured the surface vegetation and soil, hopefully exposing a vein, and creating at the foot of the hill a heap of debris which itself may have contained loose ore which could readily be obtained.

A vein thus revealed was worked by driving a level, or adit, along it into the hillside, the first few yards passing through soft ground being protected with a masonry arch and short tunnel. Many such openings can now be identified across the ore-field. Adits were invariably driven with a slight upwards incline to help drain away the water that was always one of the biggest problems facing lead miners in the late eighteenth and early nineteenth centuries.

Since most veins were several feet wide they could be worked upwards and downwards simultaneously. As the ore was extracted from above, false wooden floors could be inserted on a timber framework, with access to various working faces on a vein by means of stemples, wooden pegs driven into the side walls. The cavity left by the mining and extraction of ore was called a stope.

Working a vein by means of levels rather than by shafts sunk along it had three advantages. First, the hilly nature of the mining-field made it possible to drive levels from valley sides, resulting in easier extraction; second, a level near the valley floor would drain all levels above it and in so doing would collect sufficient head of water to work machinery for pumping out even lower levels, and third, long levels could easily strike new veins during their course of construction. It is known that levels were being driven in the Alston Moor ore field by 1737, but it was Coalcleugh, at the head of West Allendale, that claimed the first horse-drawn waggonway along an underground level a mile long in 1765. Such long levels as this were intended to 'unwater' a whole series of mines, and it was Sopwith's ambitious Blackett Level, commenced in 1855, that eventually reached the astonishing length of four-and-a-half miles. The entrance to this can still be seen in Allendale Town, below the church at the confluence of a small stream with the East Allen. The first edition of the Ordnance Survey Map, surveyed in 1859 and published in 1865, does not show this. It was intended to have been nearly seven miles long, with four shafts sunk on to it from the surface, but by 1903 the Allenheads mine had closed, the collapse of the local industry was complete, and the Blackett Level remained unfinished.

The driving of levels and the sinking of shafts was done by miners known as deadmen or sappers. Pickmen worked the vein, using picks, hammers and oak wedges to crack the rock and shovels to shift it, by the light of candles standing in clay. Both groups worked in small teams or partnerships, the organisation and control of which was governed by the 'bargain' system between employer and employed, during the eighteenth and nineteenth centuries. Conditions changed very little during that period, and an 1842 report stated that:

> The miners with few exceptions, speculate on the produce of the mines in which they work. Four miners . . . form a partnership together, and they make a bargain that they will work in a certain part of a certain mine for the next three months, for so many shillings for every bing of ore (8cwt:407kg): the expense of washing and cleaning the ore, and making it fit for the furnace, being charged to them. All the other men in the mine, in parties of 4, 5 or 6, or more, make bargains in the same way. These bargains are entered into a book, and the miners sign them.

The advantages for the mine owners was that the bargain system meant payment by results, a piecework system which encouraged miners to work hard. Initially, of course, the miners had to speculate just as much as their employers did. However, miners working a rich vein received less per bing than those on a poor vein, so that they did not necessarily share in good times as they had to do when things were bad and it became uneconomic to work poor veins.

Ore brought out of a mine was invariably mixed with other minerals – barite, fluorite, limestone, collectively known as 'bouse'. This was tipped into a stone hopper, or 'bousestead', and as many groups of miners would be working in one mine it was essential that their loads of ore and bouse were kept separate, so ranges of bousesteads were built, each with one stonewalled bay to each partnership. A particularly good example survives at Allenheads, in spite of some destruction by recent developments. Dating from 1857 it was built by Thomas Sopwith, chief mining agent of the Beaumont family enterprise from 1845–71, and across its high-stepped dividing walls ran wooden supports for a narrow-gauge rail track used by trucks carrying ore from the mines.

After collection at the bousesteads the bouse-ore mixture was crushed and washed in running water to separate the galena from the lighter waste material. Where crushing was relatively easy it was done by women and children using small hand-hammers called buckers. Tougher and less brittle ore necessitated mechanical force, which, from about 1820, took the form of a crushing mill, using heavy rollers powered by the drive from a waterwheel. Only one crushing plant survives in the entire northern ore-field and this 1870 example has been preserved and restored as part of an open-air museum and picnic site at Killhope in upper Weardale, five miles south-west of Allenheads. The 33ft (10m) diameter wheel and adjoining stone mill form a dramatic group in a lonely, austere landscape. The Killhope Works were owned by the Beaumont Company, and after crushing and dressing, the Weardale ore was carried by packhorse to Allenheads for smelting. Ore-washing, at its simplest, consisted of using flowing water in sieves, tanks and troughs, together with moving mechanisms, to separate grades of ore until the resultant galena was sufficiently pure for smelting.

Thus, water played an important role in the various processes up to this stage. A series of reservoirs with a total capacity of over sixty million gallons provided the water power for the Allenheads mine, its dressing floors and the smelt mill. What can be seen today was mainly the work of Thomas Sopwith, a friend of the great hydraulics engineer William Armstrong, so it is not surprising that he, too, was brilliant in making repeated use of the same water. Corbitmere Dam, on the high moors above Rookhope Head a mile east of Allenheads was one of the main reservoirs. Water from there was piped down the Corbitmere shaft and along the Fawside Level to two underground pumping engines, and then, after use on the dressing floors, was led back into the Allenheads Mine. Subsequently it powered four waterwheels at various levels below the village. The Dodd and Smelt Mill reservoirs supplied water for the Allenheads smelt mill before draining, like the rest of the used water, into the East Allen, subsequently to power eight more waterwheels, four of them on corn mills in the valley, and finally drove the machinery for the Allen smelt mill below Allendale Town.

Between 1729 and 1896, levels and shafts around the upper valleys of the East and West Allen rivers yielded over a quarter of a million tons of lead concentrates. Lead mining and smelting in the Allendales was dominated by the Blackett and Beaumont families since the late seventeenth century. The Blacketts owned the rich mine at Burtree Pasture in upper Weardale, at Coalcleugh at the head of West Allendale, at Allenheads, together with smelt mills at Allenheads, Allendale Town, Dukesfield, Dirt Pot and in Weardale. The Allenheads smelt mill, now vanished, was built by the Blacketts in the early eighteenth century, and by 1821 incorporated three ore hearths, a roasting furnace and a slag hearth.

An ore hearth was similar to a blacksmith's hearth, with the hearth itself about 2ft (.6m) square and 1ft (.3m) deep placed beneath an arched masonry hood spanning perhaps 12ft (3.6m), and with a depth of 6ft

(1.8m), thus allowing working space at the sides and front. Behind was a bellows-room, where water-powered bellows drove air through openings in the masonry called 'tuyeres', into the hearth.

The cast-iron hearth with its integral, projecting grooved workstone sloping from one side, was supported in strongly-built masonry. Using coal or peat as fuel, ore was heated in a current of air, its impurities burnt off as gases, and the residual molten metal run off, first into preheated cast-iron sumpter pots which were subsequently tapped, the ore ladled into moulds, the resultant pigs of lead each weighing about 1¼ cwts.

Grey slag produced by the ore hearth contained a mixture of oxides of lead, carbonaceous ash, lime and other impurities, but still retained sufficient lead content to be regarded as low-grade ore. This was resmelted in a slag hearth, which resembled an ore-hearth without the workstone, and used coke as fuel, necessitating a stronger blast. Fifteen to twenty per cent of lead was recovered this way, leaving a black, vitreous slag. Ore hearth and slag hearth smelting were relatively small-scale processes suited to small partnerships of men dealing with small parcels of ore; nevertheless, smelters were specialists, very skilled workmen, during the eighteenth and nineteenth centuries, and at no time were boys used in this job. To maximise efficiency furnaces needed to be kept going for long periods at a time, with occasional stops for cooling, so smelters worked long hours, with the normal duration of a shift at an ore-hearth of twelve to fifteen hours. An 1831 report describes this well:

> At mills where the smelting shift is 12 hours, the hearths usually go on 12 hours and are suspended 5 . . . the two who manage the hearth, each work four shifts per week; terminating their week's work on Wednesday afternoon. They are succeeded by two other men, who also work four 12 hour shifts, the last of which they finish at four o'clock on Saturday. In these eight shifts from 36-40 bings of ore are smelted (14-20 tonnes) which, when of good quality, produce from 9-10 fodders of lead (one fodder was 21 cwts). At other mills where the shift is from fourteen to fifteen hours, the furnace is kindled at four o'clock in the morning, and worked until six or seven in the evening each day, six days in the week . . . Two men at one hearth, in the early part of each week, work three such shifts, producing about 4 fodders of lead . . . two other men work each three shifts in the latter part of the week . . .

Although there were permutations in the number of hours worked, the results were the same: each smelter worked long shifts, followed by a good break of three or four days before the next set of shifts.

At the time of the Report quoted a smelter's pay seemed to average 7s per fodder of lead, and it only rarely exceeded 14-15s a week. But smelting, like ore-dressing, was not a full-time job, being affected by seasonal influences. During really cold weather in winter not only would ore-washing cease, but the packhorse and carrier tracks from mines to smelt-mill became impassable. Fuel for the hearths became more scarce, and hard frosts froze the water supply to the wheels powering bellows. Alternative labour on the land was often introduced, such as cutting new drainage channels, repairing walls and dams, and laying hedges.

Lead-mining was hazardous and unhealthy, while smelting incurred risk of poisoning from the fumes and gases which the process produced. Sometime in the early nineteenth century long horizontal flues were introduced to the north Pennine ore-field. These were sometimes as much as half-a-mile long, built of good masonry, in the form of an arched tunnel on the surface of the land, usually slanting up a hillside from the smelt mill to a terminal stack on the crest of a moor, removing the noxious fumes from the smelt mill and the area around it. Mainly intended to recover the vapourised lead which sublimed on their inner surfaces, they certainly improved ventilation for the smelting process and made working conditions less unhealthy. The two terminal stacks seen prominently on the moors between Allendale Town and West Allendale, 8153, are at the ends of a complicated series of flues from the Allen mill at Catton. Constructed between 1845 and 1850 under the guidance of Thomas Sopwith, one of them is 4,451yd (4070m) long, the other 4,338yd (3967m), the combined length of about 5 miles (8km) far exceeds any other mill flue system in the country, much of it still traceable on the ground.

Some ores were rich in silver, and it was important that the ore from silver-rich veins was kept separated from poorer quality material. In the 1830s, Hugh Lee Pattinson, who worked for various north Pennine mining companies during his career, invented a more satisfactory process for refining silver-rich lead than had hitherto existed. This involved re-melting pigs of lead and then letting them cool very slowly. The lead crystallised before the silver and was removed with a perforated ladle, leaving behind richer lead. The process was repeated until eventually pure silver was left. One tonne of lead could be expected to yield up to 5oz (190g) of silver.

During the eighteenth and nineteenth centuries most of the population of the Allendales and the upper Derwent valley depended directly or indirectly on lead mining for a living. The mines were worked either by a landowner who had the mining rights, as with the Blackett and Beaumont families who owned the rights in Allendale, or were leased by a landowner to concessionaires. The title of Lord of the Manor in Allendale was held by the Blackett family of Wallington until 1792, when it passed to the Beaumonts, through an illegitimate daughter.

During the eighteenth century the Derwent mines were worked by the Quaker London Lead Company, but in the following century by the Derwent Mining Company. Mention must also be made of the

Commissioners of Greenwich Hospital for Seamen who, in 1734, were granted much of the confiscated northern estates of the Jacobite Earl of Derwentwater. These included mineral rights on the Alston Moor orefield, subsequently leased to the London Lead Company on a royalty basis. In 1768 the Greenwich Hospital Commissioners built their own smelt mill at Langley, between Haydon Bridge and Allendale Town, and this continued working until 1833 when it passed into the hands of a private company, Shield and Dinning, until its final closure in 1887.

Little remains of the Langley smelt mill, although local farm buildings reveal traces. The course of its remarkable flue can be traced, zig-zagging its way south-eastwards up the hillside to its terminal chimney, 841611, south of the B6305 on Stublick Moor. Stublick Farm, to the south-west, 833605, incorporates many of the well-built and well-maintained mine buildings of the small Stublich Colliery, developed largely to provide coal for the Langley smelt mill. At Langley Byers, 831612, a number of small, enclosed fields represent the allotments given to smelters in the late eighteenth century as an inducement to work in the smelt mill.

Indeed, throughout the north Pennine area the land was too poor and the climate too harsh for arable farming, but apart from the normal service industries and trades there was no alternative work to lead mining and its associated jobs. Many lead mining families had small-holdings – some of the companies actively encouraged this dual economy – although most were too small to sustain a full-time employment on the land. Sopwith's report of 1857 states, 'There are very few purely agricultural labourers; most of the farms are occupied by miners and smelters, and people connected with those works'. A miner's cottage was often, in effect, a farmstead with living quarters, barn and hayloft all under a single roof. The Allendales, in particular towards the valley-heads where the mines were situated, show the dispersed settlement pattern of cottages and fields.

The Beaumonts' Allendale estates were surveyed and mapped in 1861 (under Sopwith's direction of course). This showed that in the Coalcleugh area twenty-five out of the forty-four houses owned enclosed meadow or pasture land, while at Allenheads the proportion was 81 out of 123 (57 per cent and 66 per cent respectively). Acreages varied between one and ten, most being of over five acres, which included a bigger proportion of pasture than meadow. This dual economy was possible because miners worked relatively short hours. By the middle of the nineteenth century five, eight-hour shifts, sometimes five, six-hour shifts, seems to have been the usual in Beaumont mines, each day's work starting at seven or eight am. This, during the seven better months of the year, left miners plenty of daylight hours to work on the small-holdings. Those miners who lived away from home in mine-shops during the week were able to arrange their shifts to allow them to finish on Friday mornings, thus enabling them to have 'long' weekends at home. No adult miners normally worked on Saturdays or Sundays during the eighteenth and nineteenth centuries.

An additional facility on the Beaumont estates was that miners were allowed a few days' holiday at the time of hay harvest (late July and August in a good season), while children in the Beaumont schools were given five weeks' holiday at that time.

From their small-holdings lead miners gained not only a useful quantity of food but a pleasant, open-air, healthy contrast to conditions of work in mines and mills. Security against hard times was an additional advantage, while the mine-owners and landlords benefited through being able to let land which would otherwise probably have been merely left waste. Of additional importance was the fact that miners' small-holdings helped to secure a workforce to a particular district and landlord.

Small-holdings were devoted only to grass, grazed by stock to provide food and transport. Most miners had at least one cow, for milk, butter and cheese. Summer grazing would be moorland commons or in enclosed rough pasture; in winter cows were fed on hay and kept on enclosed land, or more likely in a barn. Geese, being grazers, were common, together with bees, which enjoyed the moorland heather. Pigs and poultry were rarely kept since the potatoes and cereals they would require were of more importance to miners themselves. A few goats rather than sheep were not uncommon, while the strong and hardy Dales ponies were a necessity, to serve the miner and his family for transport or for pulling a cart.

Transport was important to lead miners: it was vital in the industry itself, and a good part of the labour force was directly concerned with it. Ore had to be carried from mines to smelt mills, as of course did fuel. Pig lead had to be carried from mills to the lead markets, which, for most of the north Pennine mills meant Newcastle, and the transport costs in the eighteenth century when roads were so appalling loomed large in the economy of lead production. The Blackett company spent more on transport than on smelting.

In the years of pre-industrial transport, packhorses – usually 'galloways' – formed the basis of the system until better roads were made, and the railways were introduced, and continued as the main form of local transport until lead mining ended. A report of 1768 refers to how, 'The Ore is carried from the Mines to the Mills entirely on Horseback; Galloways being employed carrying two Pokes of Ore, each weighing 1cwt, that is ⅛ of a Bing, consequently a Bing is carried by 4 Galloways'. By 1805 ore was being taken to Langley smelt mill either on galloways or on one-horse carts which carried one bing.

The carriers were usually small farmers, often tenants of the mining companies, using the carrying trade to supplement their income. Later in the period they tended to concentrate on carrying, keeping an increasing stock of galloways as the only stock grazing their land. Many carriers lived on the edge of the mining area, particularly those of the Greenwich Hospital Company, who seemed to have been concentrated around Hexham. Administration of the carriers was in the hands of the mining agents of the companies concerned, and was a complex business presenting many problems, not least caused by the weather. Frequently, pigs of lead had to be stored or left by the roadside, as Cobbett observed in 1832 (*Tour in Scotland*) between Hexham and Newcastle, commenting on 'loads of these pigs lying by the roadside . . . no fear of their being stolen: their weight is their security'.

Today, the tracks used by these galloways and packhorse trains can be followed over the moors of Hexhamshire and Allendale. One such is the well-defined Broad Way running north-north-eastwards from Allenheads up Byerhope Bank, Tedham Moss and Lilswood Moor where it becomes an enclosed lane to join the minor road to Whitley Chapel before crossing Devil's Water to the Dukesfield Smelt Mill. There, all that survives of an important and prosperous mill are two huge 'Gothic' arches which probably carried the flues from the furnace. Other carriers' routes running eastwards and north-eastwards from Allendale start as walled lanes before crossing the open moorlands of Westburnhope, Eshels, Spitalshield and Greenrigg, leading to the Devil's Water or Hexham.

# 6
# ROADS, TRACKS AND RAILWAYS

### Roads and Tracks

Over much of the Northumbrian uplands an intricate pattern of ancient tracks, green lanes, drove roads and bridlepaths stitches the spacious landscape with threads spanning thirty centuries. They offer, especially to walkers, a unique blend of history and splendid scenery, and although the military training area around Redesdale imposes restrictions, many miles of rights-of-way exist along routes used by prehistoric man journeying between hill forts, by pastoral Celts, by Scottish drovers. They may be faint shadows on the grass, hollow ways in the heather, walled lanes, forestry roads, or tarred modern roads such as Dere Street, but each has a rich humus of communication and culture.

Dere Street itself probably follows an older route. The Cheviots, especially along their lower margins, show evidence of considerable prehistoric settlement, particularly during the five centuries before the Romans arrived, and there would have been some connecting network of tracks. Commenting on trackways in the Border area the Royal Commission on the Ancient Monuments of Scotland in its Roxburgh volume states that 'in their choice of routes they affect high-lying ground, avoiding valleys and deep cleughs; the hazards and difficulties of swampy ground and peat hags having evidently been preferred to those of woods, screes and torrents.' Since the topography of Cheviot landscape is similar on both sides of the Border line, and has not changed since prehistoric times, man and his stock will have continued to use routes which themselves will have changed little over the centuries since then. They will have crossed rivers and streams, and the high ridges, at the same

points. Not only on the Cheviots but also on the Simonside hills above
Rothbury, shadowy tracks in the grass, or trenched ruts in the heather,
have a long history of human use. The chain of hill forts between
Kirknewton and Wooler is linked along the Cheviots' southern slopes by
a series of trackways, now enjoyed by walkers who prefer the quiet, secret
places among the hills, between the College and Humbleton Burns.

From the Coquet valley at Barrow Burn, 867107, a green track marked
on the map as 'The Street' climbs steadily north-westwards, crosses the
Cheviot ridge near Mozie Law, 835150, and descends to the Kale Water
at Hownam, 778191. Although it is known to have been in use in the late
nineteenth century for packhorse traffic and even more recently for the
carriage of loads of oatmeal from Scotland to isolated Northumbrian
shepherds in the hills, it was probably used by drovers in the eighteenth
century, while a possible reference in a twelfth-century charter suggests
an earlier importance. A closer examination of parts of 'The Street' has
shown that some of its ruts overlie an older track less than 20ft (6m)
across. But it is virtually impossible to ascribe a date to this; it could be of
Dark Age origin, its name hints at Roman associations, it could be far
older still. No matter how deep its historical humus, it remains one of the
most exhilarating tracks for present-day walkers to explore and savour the
splendour of Cheviot country.

A few miles to the east Clennell Street, probably the best-known of
the Cheviot 'streets', was never Romanised, but had a long trading
tradition as a route linking Scotland with the more prosperous lands on
the English side of the Border, as well as the Northumbrian outposts of
the Votadini with their tribal headquarters to the north. Newminster
monks used it to reach their upland sheep pastures on Kidland, and it was
named in a monastic charter of 1181 as 'the great road of Yarnspeth', a
description which surely implies a long usage. Running from Alwinton to
Cocklawfoot, 854185, in the valley of the Bowmont Water, it was almost
certainly favoured during the Border troubles by cattle reivers from both
sides, and in later centuries was used by southbound Scottish drovers with
their cattle, and, more clandestinely, by whisky smugglers distributing
the precious products of Rory's Still near Uswayford. The Ordnance
Survey identifies Clennell Street in the Gothic script reserved for non-
Roman antiquities, whereas The Street is printed normally. Dere Street,
by contrast, is backed both ways, named in Gothic script, and also
described as Roman Road. Near Chew Green it is called (in Gothic)
'Gamel's Path', probably a medieval name.

Dere Street, however, was not the first Roman road in
Northumberland. That distinction goes to the Stanegate, the strategic
supply route between Corstopitum (Corbridge) and Carlisle, begun in
AD80 and completed about twenty years later. It forms the main east-
west thoroughfare within Corstopitum, but its course is then very sketchy

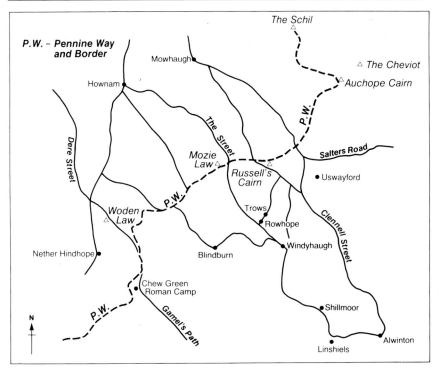

**Some Border 'Streets'**

until the village of Newbrough, 875678, is reached, where a minor modern road follows its alignment for many miles to the west. This soon climbs to higher ground at Settlingstones, and in another mile, at the crossroads on Grindon Hill, 830680, the Stanegate forms the southern boundary of the National Park, and though used by modern traffic, the 27ft (8.2m) wide agger, raised about 2ft (.6m) above the adjoining land, is easily identified.

Near Crindledykes the modern road swings southwards, but the Stanegate continues across the fields to Chesterholm, where it passes along the north side of the fort, Vindolanda. A fine cylindrical Roman milestone, in situ, stands in a quiet grove by the stream crossing. Beyond the stream the road is a hollow way, but soon rises to its agger again, past another broken milestone. Beyond the metalled road leading northward to the Twice Brewed Inn it becomes a farm road to Seatside and crosses rough ground to join the main road B6318 near the standing stones known as The Mare and Foal, 726664. From there, Stanegate apparently continues westwards, almost parallel to the main road but just to its north, through fields, behind Fell End Farm, and leading to the fort at Carvoram (Magna), where it is quite close to the Wall. Beyond there, although its course has been traced, very little can be seen.

Dere Street is the post-Roman name given to the road built from AD80 onwards, following Agricola's advance into Scotland from Corbridge. The modern road A68 picks up the Roman line a few hundred yards north of the intersection with the new course of the Newcastle-Carlisle road, A69, a mile north-west of Corbridge, and maintains a close alignment for most of the 24 miles to High Rochester. The only significant deviations are near Colwell, where it crosses the Dry Burn, 940764, between Fourlaws, 906827, and Woodhouse, 889873, and at Elishaw a few miles farther north. At each of these deviations the Roman road can be easily recognised where it crosses rough ground. To the left of the modern road where it breasts the hill north of West Woodburn, a Roman milestone has recently been re-erected by the Redesdale Local History Society. From there to its junction with the A696 at Elishaw, Dere Street and the A68 form part of the eastern boundary of the National Park.

No place on Dere Street evokes the frontier nature of Northumberland so convincingly as the Portgate on Stagshaw Bank, where it crosses the line of Hadrian's Wall, and the much later 'military road' of General Wade's construction of 1752 still creates a crossroads of sufficient size and importance to merit an enormous roundabout by the Errington Arms. There in Roman times north-bound convoys of troops and officials would leave the relative safety of the zone protected by the Wall for the wild frontier hills of Cheviot country to the north, haze-blue in the far distance. And there, in the great cattle-droving days of the eighteenth and early nineteenth centuries, Scottish drovers and their beasts assembled at the stances on Stagshaw Bank for the great fairs which were held there, the site to the west of Dere Street now marked by gorse bushes and coarse, wind-bent grasses.

At Blakehope, 857946, the A68 turns sharply north-eastwards to the A696 junction at Elishaw, leaving the Roman road continuing along a north-western alignment, detectable in the fields as a narrow strip of distinctively-coloured vegetation. Its course is lost near the river but has been identified at Horsley, continuing to the fort Bremenium, at High Rochester. Beyond, Dere Street takes a more northerly orientation, past a series of Roman temporary camps above the Sills Burn, through a modern military training area, to Featherwood Farm. Here, it kinks eastwards before returning to a northerly, then north-westerly course, as Gamel's Path, to the Chew Green camps and the Border line on Brownhart Law, 1,663ft (507m), where its course has been adopted for a mile by the Pennine Way. Beyond Greystone Brae Dere Street swings away westwards to Woden Law and Pennymint, leaving the Pennine Way to its airy route along the Cheviot crests.

Another Roman road, known as the Devil's Causeway, left Dere Street at Beukley, 982708, north of the Portgate, and continued northwards to Berwick, largely outside our area, and these two split the main Celtic areas of Northumbrian settlement. A link between them was provided by a lateral road between High Rochester and Low Learchild, 093112, near Whittingham. Although its course is marked on the map, and has been identified for most of its length, it is neither easily seen nor readily explored, except in a few places. Probably the best-known of these is at Lady's Well, Holystone, 953028, where it has emerged as a track from Campville Wood, and running north-eastwards across the Harbottle road, approaches the River Coquet as an artificial cutting in the river terrace. To the north-east, near Callaly, the present road is on or very close to the Roman line through woodland. Significantly, the cottages at the western end of the woods are called Street Way.

No roads were constructed in this area between Roman times and the middle of the eighteenth century, and there is little historical evidence for any medieval roads in the uplands of north and west Northumberland. Any journeys by Norman and medieval kings and nobles seem to have been from Newcastle to Berwick via Morpeth, Alnwick and the coastal plain, or to Carlisle via Hexham and the Tyne Gap. These are the only Northumbrian routes shown in Ogilby's *British Roads* of 1675.

Even in an area so thinly settled as that now within the National Park, and in the moorlands south of the Tyne, some movement of humans and livestock will have occurred. Communications between villages and hamlets, between farms, fortified houses, and local markets and fairs, slowly evolved in piecemeal fashion as rough tracks. Some have become the motor roads of today, especially in the two Tyne valleys; others have vanished, or have survived only as public footpaths and bridleways often very difficult to follow. Specific commodities were carried such as monastic wool from outlying granges of Newminster Abbey, either to the Abbey itself at Morpeth, or directly to the port of Newcastle. Salt formed important loads on packhorses which carried it inland from coastal saltpans such as those known to exist at Blyth. One hill-road crossing the Cheviot illustrates this traffic.

At Alnham the Salters' Road, named on the map, climbs as a grassy track past the church and pele tower, heading north-westwards along the flanks of High Knowes to Shank House, 961135, to cross the upper River Breamish at Bleakhope, 926157, before crossing a watershed between Bloodybush Edge and Lint Lands. It then drops into the narrow valley of the Clay Burn, where a branch goes down to Uswayford, while the main trade route continued westwards, over the Usway Burn at Davidson's Linn, to join Clennell Street on the Border ridge, and its subsequent descent to Cocklawfoot and a route to Jedburgh.

Except where river or stream crossings were too deep for packhorses safely to ford them, bridges were scarcely necessary for the traffic of medieval times. The existence of an ancient bridge thus indicates there was probably a well-used track leading to an important river crossing at that point. Within our area only a handful of bridges indicates such river crossings before the sixteenth century. Haydon Bridge is the only place between Newcastle and Carlisle where the old road crossed the Tyne, and a bridge is mentioned there in a number of fourteenth-century documents. But like others spanning the Tyne, it was destroyed in the great flood of 1771, and the present stone structure dates from 1773, with some rebuilding and widening since then.

Linnels Bridge, with its single segmental arch of 45ft (13.7m) spanning the Devil's Water south of Hexham, probably dates from 1698, although a worn inscription dating it to 1581 may have come from its predecessor. Rothbury bridge may also have fifteenth- or sixteenth-century origins, although it was widened on the downstream side by six feet, probably in 1760 and more recent unsightly widening for footways beyond the parapets has made it even more difficult to pick out the four chamfered ribs beneath each of its segmental arches. You need to walk the riverside footpath to obtain the most satisfying view of this feature, and its good sandstone masonry. The riverside path at Corbridge also provides the best viewpoint for the splendid seven-arched bridge of 1674 which alone survived the 1771 floodwaters of a surging river whose level was so high that people could wash their hands in the water merely by leaning over the parapet. A bridge at Corbridge was first recorded in 1235, but in 1361 was said to be 'broken down'. It must have been repaired by the time of Leland's visit about 1540, when the remains of a Roman bridge were quite substantial.

The North Tyne can still claim the most impressive survival of a Roman bridge abutment. This is on the east side of the river opposite Chesters fort (Cilurnum), reached by a ½ mile (800m) footpath from the B6318 at Chollerford Bridge. Over the centuries since the Romans built their timber bridge, probably in the third century, the river has changed its course, burying the eastern abutment and the pier nearest to it in the river bank from where it was uncovered in 1860. The massive masonry is now high and dry, on a polygonal base whose enormous size suggests that it once supported a very strong superstructure.

The nature of the land, as well as political factors, has dictated that the general orientation of roads in Northumberland is north-south, and north-west to south-east. The main exception is the east-west road through the Tyne Gap. The A68 is the only important road which crosses the Cheviot range, and it is 24 crow-flying miles from Carter Bar to the A697 at Wooler, where this eases past the flanks of the hills. Eight miles south-east of Carter Bar the minor road beyond Kielder joins the B6357 at Saughtree, probably following an old route mentioned in a survey of 1543. This gave seventeen crossings of the Cheviots, which, working from east to west, are:

1. White Swire
2. Pete Swire
3. Auchope Rig, between Auchope Cairn and the Schil
4. Hunt Road (probably over Butt Roads, 1,718ft (524m) 3 miles south-west of the Cheviot
5. Hexpethgate (the Clennell Street route)
6. Maiden Cross (near Windy Gyle)
7. Black Braes (along The Street)
8. Hindmoor Well (over Lamb Hill)
9. Hewghen Gate (probably Greystone Brae, north of Chew Green)
10. Gamel's Path
11. Almond Road (over Whiteside Hill and Coquet Head)
12. Phillip's Cross (not in 1543 list, but named in 1597). This is now marked by a cairn on Catcleugh Hill, 746066
13. Redeswire (the present Carter Bar road)
14. Carter-Carter Fell (this crosses the Border 4 miles SW of Carter Bar, at Knox Knowe, 655027
15. Wheel Causeway (named in Gothic script, in Wauchope Forest, crosses the Border at 606980, just north of Deadwater)
16. Bells (the road, Saughtree-Deadwater)
17. Kershopehead, east of Newcastleton, 545865

It is known that in 1296 Edward I travelled along the Wheel Causeway, while the Redeswire crossing now adopted by the main Carter Bar road has a similar proven antiquity, and is mentioned in a 1375 account. Eighteenth-century maps, including Roy's Military Survey of Scotland 1750, refer to Dere Street as the 'road from Jedburgh', and Clennell Street is described as the 'road from Morpeth to Kelso'. Wheel Causeway is also named as the 'road to Jedburgh', and much of its course today is through Wauchope Forest, identifiable as a broad forest ride from 659053 southwards to Wheelrig Head, beyond which its course is very hard to follow, but can be picked up again south of the Border, as a bridleway descending the spur north of Deadwater. Armstrong's map of 1768 names as the Jedburgh Road the track leaving the North Tyne at Falstone, heading north-west over Hawkhope to Kielder Head, 666980, (mainly forest tracks today), then northwards by the western flanks of Kielderhead Moor to the Border crossing at Knox Knowe, descending on the Scottish side through Wauchope Forest to the present A6088. This, and most of the tracks on the Tudor list, can be traced on Sheet 80, 'Cheviot Hills and Kielder Forest area', which in its northern half, embracing most of the Cheviots north and east of the A68, shows a magnificently roadless landscape.

Tracks north of the Border are shown as black broken lines which, on a map so crowded with contours, stand out very distinctly. Their continuation on the English side is usually in red, indicating public footpaths or bridleways, and between Carter Bar and Auchope Cairn at least ten of the Border crossings can be identified, while all of those to the west of Carter Bar are given. To explore any, some, or all of them is stimulating, exhilarating and rewarding. Their green tracks provide the best walking in Border country, mainly on surfaces good for walking, with a rich mixture of scenic variety, historic interest, usually easy to follow, and as challenging as you care to make them. I prefer them in early spring or late autumn, when the bracken is neither waist-high nor monotonously green and fly-haunted, and when the lower angle of sunlight models the contours and etches the surface features of the past, and visibility, especially in a breezy north-westerly, stretches to horizons scores of miles away – 'Trevelyan weather', you might describe it.

Alwinton was a junction of two important historic Border crossings, Clennell Street and The Street. This fact, together with its being a centre for a widely-scattered population of the Cheviots, has given it an importance disproportionate to its size. The name of its old-fashioned pub, The Rose and Thistle, one of the best in Border country, refers to the Union of Crowns, and is a reminder that the Border is only a few miles away, seven in fact, for a high-flying Cheviot crow, a little more by way of Clennell Street. However, by starting farther up the Coquet valley at Windyhaugh, 866109, you can sample these two ancient routes in a circular walk of nine miles which also incorporates part of the Pennine Way along the crest of the Cheviots.

If Alwinton was the Coquetdale focus for Cheviot crossings nearby, Elsdon performed a similar function for tracks converging on Redesdale. Apart from Dere Street four miles to the west, probably the most important track, certainly used in droving days, is that running south-eastwards from Chew Green, named as Gamel's Path for its first few miles, but then, near Featherwood, swinging eastwards from Dere Street, and winding across the moors now in the Military Area, past Bushman's Crag, 844036, and Bluestone Edge before straightening on a south-easterly alignment across Daryshiel Common and Leighton Hill. It may have entered the village along the line of a field path coming in from the west, or by the present B6341, which was the old route linking Elsdon with the main part of its parish in Redesdale.

These moors between upper Coquetdale and Redesdale, military-dominated today, have for centuries provided a relatively easy corridor of communications between the rich lands of the Tweed valley and the heart of Northumberland. Medieval tracks, raiders' tracks and drovers' tracks have threaded their way south-eastwards. Named landmarks perhaps commemorate people who travelled that way, Saddlers Knowe, Ridlees Cairn, Foulplay Knowe, but one of the best-known, the Pedlar's Stone, 935005, marking the junction of tracks between Redesdale and Coquetdale, has vanished, a victim of the military.

Drovers bound for Newcastle and Tyneside would have continued south-eastwards from Elsdon or the Coquet valley along routes which are represented by modern roads leading out of our area. Those heading southwards favoured Dere Street, to the site of the important fair at Stagshaw Bank, and the steep descent to the Tyne valley, where droving traffic concentrated at the fords at Corbridge and Riding Mill. At Corbridge the old approach to the ford is indicated by the narrow passage down Spout Well Lane, leading down to the river from the eastern end of Main Street. Using this crossing enabled the drovers to avoid paying tolls at the bridge.

South of the Tyne the course of the drovers' route has been lost beneath farmland and afforestation, but its course can be picked up again near Slaley. At Spring House, 958560, now surrounded by the conifer plantations of Slaley Forest, there was a stance for cattle, while the drovers were given a bed of hay in the byres. The drovers' road is now a forest road, but on emerging from the trees it continues southwards as a well-defined track over Acton Fell and Blanchland Moor to Pennypie House, 950518, formerly an inn, and the Derwent valley at Baybridge west of Blanchland, where it left Northumberland for the moors of west Durham.

The old Border crossing by the Wheel Causeway was a favourite one for drovers, who continued down the North Tyne valley to Falstone, beyond which its course has become obscured by forests. It probably crossed the Roman Wall near Housesteads, continued southwards over Thorngrafton Common, and forded the South Tyne near Whitechapel, where there was a smithy. It continued up Allendale by Staward and Allenheads, and over the high moors to Weardale and beyond.

One more drovers' route is worth mentioning because it utilised a Roman road. From Hawick its course was by way of Riccarton and the Larriston Fells, southwards close to the Border line, to Christianbury Crag, 567822, and the Bewcastle Fells; all this now lost in afforestation. In his novel *The Two Drovers* Sir Walter Scott refers to 'Christianbury Crag' and 'The Waste', now Spadeadam Waste. This part of its course is in Cumbria, but the drovers' route, keeping to the line of the Roman road, entered Northumberland at Gilsland, where it followed the Stanegate eastwards to the fort at Carvoram (Magnis). Southwards from here the route crosses Featherstone Common, and is then represented by a narrow road through Burnfoot and Greenriggs, and crosses the main A689 near Lambley, 666586. From there, over the lower slopes of Hartleyburn Common and Glendue Fell, the Maiden Way (Roman road) and drove road have been adopted for three miles by the Pennine Way, its historic past recognised in the hollow way sections, and by its broad agger on parts of the heather moor.

From Burnstones the modern main road is superimposed on the old track as far as Castle Nook, where the Maiden Way climbs to the impressive earthen ramparts of Whitley Castle, *696487*, followed by a long ascent, across the Cumbrian border, over Gilderdale Forest and the northern flanks of Cross Fell to Kirkland and Appleby in the Vale of Eden. Along this and the other routes, Scottish drovers and their dogs, driving 100-300 beasts up to 15 miles a day on the hoof, resting rough or at wayside inns, moved slowly through eighteenth- and early nineteenth-century Northumberland, making their way to the English markets of the burgeoning Midlands, many to Smithfield itself. The lonely green tracks beneath wide skies, occasional sites of overnight stances where beasts grazed, fords at burns and rivers, some village greens (as at Elsdon) and a few former drovers' inns, are their memorials. For the communities through which they passed during the summer months they brought a little income through the rent for their stances; they certainly brought stories and anecdotes from distant places, while the necessary shoeing of beasts' hooves undoubtedly made plenty of work for local smiths.

Available evidence suggests that the road system of Northumberland, such as it was, was so bad in the early eighteenth century that there was probably less wheeled traffic than at any period since monastic times four or five centuries earlier. As one historian noted, 'On the North Road rich men's coaches and carriers' wagons lumbered along at three miles an hour, but elsewhere men and goods went on horseback or not at all'. Such tracks as were in use, between villages and serving the few markets, had merely evolved.

Significantly, it was to meet a strategic military need that brought about the first scientifically engineered road since Agricola's Dere Street. In the aftermath of the 1745 Rebellion culminating in Culloden, General Wade, commander of the English forces based in Newcastle before and during the Rebellion, found it impossible to move his artillery westwards to Carlisle. The line of a new route was duly surveyed, but over five years elapsed before its promotion as a turnpike. By 1750, throughout England the growth of trade and industry, the development of agriculture and the need to move produce had brought about the creation of thousands of miles of new roads called turnpikes, each involving the investment of locally-raised capital to improve existing, or construct new, roads, in sections controlled by bars or gates across them where road users paid tolls. Turnpike trustees were prominent men prepared to invest money in such a road, with the expectation of receiving interest, in addition to the benefits of better transport. A Turnpike Act was necessary before such a road could be made.

Sir Lancelot Allgood, then sheriff of Northumberland, who lived at Nunwick, *880741*, in the North Tyne valley, was one of the promoters of the new 'military' road, described with its title, 'An Act for laying out, making, and keeping in repair a road proper for the passage of troops and carriage from the City of Carlisle to the town of Newcastle upon Tyne'. It was completed in 1753, and in the area covered by this book it is represented by the B6318, built almost on the course of the Roman Wall itself from Heddon-on-the-Wall, near Newcastle, to the North Tyne at Chollerford. Further west it deviates southwards from the line of the Wall, presenting travellers with superb views of Roman Wall landscapes particularly in its course along the southern edge of the National Park, from near Chesters to the Tipalt Burn at Greenhead. There had been a bridge at Chollerford in medieval times but the present five-arched structure carrying the Military Road over the North Tyne was designed by Mylne in 1783 to replace that lost in the 1771 floods.

The completion of Wade's road spurred a period of intensive road-building involving hundreds of miles of new roads created by a score of Turnpike Trusts over the next eighty years, and forming the basis of today's network. Again, it was Northumbrian gentry who took the lead, admittedly motivated to some extent by self-interest. The Corn Road, or 'Alemouth Turnpike', between Hexham and Alnmouth, which forms my arbitrary eastern limit to the area discussed, and now represented by the A6079, B6342 and B6341, is a splendid example of a mid-eighteenth-century turnpike.

Under contemporary Corn Laws the government provided bounties for the export of corn, should its price fall below a certain level. Rich Northumberland landowners grew vast acreages of corn, so it was sensible to improve the means of transporting it to a port for shipment. A road from Hexham to Alnmouth was the answer. The names of the subscribers to the 1753 promotion make interesting reading, together with the investments they made.

| | |
|---|---:|
| Lord Northumberland | £1,000 |
| Sir Walter Blackett | 500 |
| Sir John Swinburn | 300 |
| Sir Charles Lorraine | 300 |
| Mr Delaval | 300 |
| Mr Ridle | 300 |
| Mr Allgood | 300 |
| Mr Thornton | 300 |

The road would pass through the estates of these subscribers. Other interested investors were to subscribe a further £1,600, to create a total of £4,900. Six bridges were to be built at a total cost of £300, three toll-houses would cost £60 each, and the 24ft (7.3m) wide road was costed at £90 a mile, exclusive of bridges. With a total length of 44 miles (70.8km), the whole outlay was expected to be £4,440. Interest on money borrowed, plus a few officials' salaries, and estimated annual repair charges, brought this to just over £4,700. Thus were the relatively simple economics of creating a new road in the 1750s. The work was carried out quickly and the road soon came into being.

*Grooved track for packhorses in the Simonside Hills*

Although recent road improvements near Hexham have changed the aspects of the old road, the A6079 follows its line closely from the crossroads west of Acomb, where Armstrong's 1769 map of Northumberland indicates a 'Barr', or tollgate. But it is beyond the A68 crossroads that a journey north-eastwards along the B6342 to Rothbury evokes the character of the Corn Road, helped by the improved landscapes of eighteenth-century landlords who were the original Trustees of the promotion – Swinburnes near Colwell, Delaval at Bavington, Lorraine at Kirkharle, Blackett at Wallington. Neat hedgerows, mature trees, planted copses, and the regular accents of milestones mark the road's geometric course across the un-villaged heartlands of Northumberland. East of the A696 the road steers its way, by a series of right-angled bends, and James Paine's elegant high-arched bridge of 1760, past the Blackett estates and parkland of Wallington (National Trust). At Gallows Hill, to the north, it turns eastwards, then northwards again at Rothley crossroads. There was a toll bar at Forestburn Gate, 077963, where the 'Crown and Thistle' would be a welcome halt for earlier travellers as it is today, its name a reminder of the Border's past. Forestburn Gate also had a smithy. As it descends Garleigh Moor the Corn Road gives marvellous views northwards to Rothbury, the

Coquet valley, Cragside's woodlands and the Rimside Moors beyond, across which the old road, now B6341, continues north-eastwards, across the A697, to Alnwick and the coast. At the same time as the Corn Road pushed its way north, a road was built across country linking Elsdon to the Corn Road at Gallows Hill, then via Scots Gap and Hartburn eastwards to Morpeth and the main North Road.

By 1794, when Bailey and Culley were publishing their Agricultural Survey for Northumberland, they were able to say, 'The turnpike roads were mostly in good order; those that have an opportunity of getting whinstone, or limestone, are the best; but they certainly would be better if the surveyors ordered the stones to be broken smaller, and the roads made wider . . . it seems that the original setters-out of these roads had a predilection for climbing and descending steep banks. This is notorious on both roads upon Rimside Moor.' This referred to the Corn Road and the Northumberland section of the London to Edinburgh coach road from Newcastle to Wooler, Coldstream and Kelso, completed about 1763, and now followed for most of its original course by the popular A697. However, north of Rimside Moor crossroads the modern line is to the east of the original, now represented by a track past Rough Castle and round the eastern edge of Thrunton Wood, descending as a wide green lane to Whittingham Lane Farm and the village beyond. Minor roads continue the eighteenth-century route northwards to Glanton and Powburn where it rejoins the modern road.

Whittingham and Glanton enjoyed a far greater importance then, and in the coaching days that followed, than they do now. Glanton was largely rebuilt in the early nineteenth century, when it became a commercial centre for Glendale south of Wooler, distributing a wide range of goods brought by carrier from Newcastle to an area becoming prosperous through agriculture and quarrying, yet remaining so sparsely populated that nobody was prepared to endow a church in Glanton.

In Redesdale Otterburn was largely the result of the gradual extension northwards of the main Newcastle-Jedburgh road, now the A696, from Kirkharle over the wastes of Ottercops Moss into Redesdale. With two Turnpike Trusts affected progress was slow, but by 1830 the Carter Bar route to Scotland was being envisaged as a rival to the main North Road via Berwick. A survey of northern roads was carried out by Telford and Rennie, but the ultimate choice through Otterburn was based on T. Sopwith's survey of 1829 for the Elsdon Trust. Toll houses were built at Knowesgate, Monkridge Hall and Whitelee, a mile south of Carter Bar. The road was completed well enough by 1841 that it was being used by through coaches from Newcastle to Edinburgh, with 'The Percy Arms' at Otterburn an important staging-post. The 'Chevy Chase' and 'Blucher' carried passengers and mail, but travelling conditions would have been uncomfortable to say the least. In fact, the proprietor of 'Chevy Chase' was allowed to pay only half the normal toll charges during winter months. The new road by-passed Elsdon, whose focal importance in Redesdale declined, and even the 'short cut' connection to the new road at Raylees, completed about 1865, made little difference.

It was not until 1833 that the present line of the A68 northwards from Corbridge received a Turnpike Act to improve it. Its promoters, meeting at 'some convenient house in Corbridge', described it as 'The Turnpike Road from the north end of the Coal Road near West Auckland (Co Durham) to the Elsdon Road near Elishaw'. After fifteen centuries, the Roman Dere Street was recognised as being ripe for improvement.

Mention has been made of the toll road from the North Tyne over the Larriston Fells into Liddesdale, constructed mainly for the carriage of coals. In Allendale it was the needs of the lead industry that brought about great improvements to local roads from 1820. Until then almost all transport had been by packhorses, but the characteristic sight of lines of galloways on valley tracks became gradually less familiar afterwards. In 1826 a new road was built from Cowshill in upper Weardale, crossing Burtree Fell and the county boundary, 853433 at 1,925ft (587m), and continuing through Allenheads and East Allendale to Allendale Town, linking up at Branchend, 851613, with the Hexham-Alston road created seventy years earlier. Although the main Hexham to Alston road from Haydon Bridge via Whitfield (now the A689) was turnpiked in 1778, with the graceful Cupola Bridge carrying it over the wooded gorge of the River Allen, 800592, built at that time, fifty years elapsed before the first coach ran as far as Alston.

### Railways

Within the area covered only one railway line survives, that between Newcastle and Carlisle, built piecemeal between 1835 and 1839, but not reaching Newcastle Central Station until the end of 1850. Its route followed the lowest ground by the Tyne valley to Hexham, and then westwards through the Tyne Gap, keeping south of the River Irthing and crossing the Eden at Wetheral. Following its success a number of other schemes were projected, but only a handful came to fruition. These were concerned with exploiting the lead-mining potential of the Alston and Allendale areas, the coal and iron workings of North Tynedale, and the agricultural riches of the central heartlands, Coquetdale, the Wansbeck valley and the Vale of Till.

Of these rural branch lines, that from Haltwhistle to Alston was the first to open (1856) and the last to close (1976). It stayed open so long mainly because there was no alternative transport route in this remote upland area during severe winter weather. Its scenic course along the South Tyne valley provided the greatest engineering challenge where it

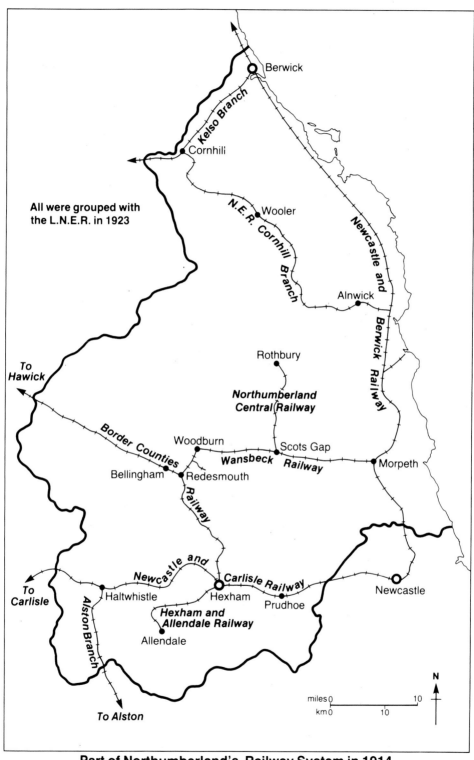

Part of Northumberland's Railway System in 1914

crossed the valley between Coanwood and Lambley on a magnificent nine-arch viaduct 110ft (33.5m) above the river, 675584, still a major focal-point in a splendid landscape setting. The Cumbrian end of this line has recently been given a new lease of life as England's highest narrow-gauge railway, and the South Tynedale Railway Preservation Society hopes to extend it from its present terminus at Gilderdale a further three miles down the valley to Slaggyford.

Opened a few years later (1869) the Hexham-Allendale line arrived just in time to see the decline of the local lead-mining industry, and never reached its intended terminus at Allenheads. Catton Road, near Allendale, was the end of the line, its station re-named 'Allendale Town' in 1898. This line never prospered, and motor-bus competition in the 1920s brought about passenger closure in 1930, with goods traffic continuing for another twenty years.

The Border Counties Railway was promoted with highest hopes although it traversed the loneliest landscapes. Coal at Plashetts and iron at Bellingham were the lure for investors' capital, and the line, opened in 1862, followed the North Tyne valley from Hexham to Riccarton Junction (beyond the Scottish border) where it joined the Border Union's Carlisle–Hawick line. Its 42 miles (67.6km) served stations at Wall, Chollerford, Chollerton, Barrasford, Wark, Redesmouth, Bellingham, Tarset, Thorneyburn, Falstone, Plashetts, Kielder, Deadwater and Saughtree. Riccarton Junction itself, 3 miles (4.8km) from the nearest road, was an extraordinary railway settlement in a wilderness, wholly dependent for its life-blood on the line.

Promoters' hopes were never realised, and the surprising thing is that the line survived until 1958 for traffic beyond Bellingham, with the Hexham–Bellingham section closing in 1963. The remarkable skew viaduct near Kielder, 632924, is its most impressive memorial, now concrete-footed and providing a scenic footpath and bridleway across Kielder Burn at the head of Bakethin Reservoir. This rare example of enlightened thinking is exceptional. The County Council has missed opportunities for saving the track-beds of former rural lines and giving them a new lease of life as walkways or cycleways, even better as linear country parks. The Haltwhistle–Alston line in particular would have provided a glorious route above the South Tyne.

Lesser rural branch lines touched the fringes of our area, and linked existing lines to the more remote agricultural regions. The Wansbeck Railway, completed in 1865, was a 25-mile (40km) link between Redesmouth and the main east-coast line at Morpeth, and reached a

(right) *Kirkharle, near Wallington*
(pp126-7) *The view to the Cheviots from Simonside*

*Lady's Well, Holystone*

height of over 850ft (260m) at Summit Cottages, *937846*, east of Ridsdale, whose ironworks and quarries provided some of its freight. Regular services ended in 1952, although for a few years afterwards special trains were run for Bellingham Fair.

From one of its intermediate stations, Scots Gap, a 13-mile (21km) spur ran northwards to Rothbury. Opened in 1870 and continuing until 1963 its leisurely service was illustrated by a journey time of 42 minutes, often including stops between stations for passengers to pick blackberries or even catch rabbits. At Rothbury and Scots Gap, auction marts built near the stations continue to flourish long after railway operations ceased. Parts of the Rothbury and Wansbeck lines have recently been incorporated by The National Trust into a 7-mile (11km) circular 'Wannie Line' walk based on Scots Gap. The people of Wooler and Glendale waited until 1887 for their railway, the Cornhill Branch from Alnwick to Cornhill-on-Tweed. Passengers continued to use the 35-mile (56km) line only until 1930, freight until 1948, when a storm breached it south of Wooler. After that it was worked in two sections, the southern one to Alnwick lasting until 1953, the northern one from Wooler at Cornhill for another twelve years. The fine viaduct at Edlingham, *117094*, and the tunnel at Hillhead, *108108*, are its best surviving works. Its well-built stone stations, as with many others on the rural lines, have subsequently become attractive private houses.

# 7
# NATURAL HISTORY

Long before life clothed and animated the landscape the underlying rocks were present, and still remain the oldest element in the natural history of the area. We have seen how they impart distinctive character to different parts, recognised in the scenic changes which occur in a journey from one part to another. Where there is gritstone and sandstone there are sombre moors, dark for much of the year but bursting into purple splendour with the flowering of the heather from mid-August. High Pennine plateaux and the Cheviot summits are, because of their impervious rocks, covered by blanket bog, but most of the Cheviots is a green landscape, far more delicate in tone and colour than that of the moorlands. Where the Whin Sill rock is near the surface, soils are too shallow to be ploughed and the old grassland is rich in plant species. In the far west, the remote and little-visited landscapes at the head of the Warks Burn and River Irthing, although covered by glacial deposits of boulder-clay, have extensive areas of peat-bog and mires with their distinctive plant communities and character. You do not need to possess the expertise of a botanist or a biologist to appreciate these scenic differences or colour contrasts, but if you recognise them and perhaps wonder why they occur you are beginning to appreciate the science of ecology and the awareness of habitats. This study of the relationship of living things to their environment and to one another is a relative newcomer. The artist

Constable would not have heard of it, nor of conservation, yet his off-quoted words 'To know is to see', although he was speaking in terms of his art, equally apply to an appreciation of natural history.

Working a generation before Constable's time, Thomas Bewick, born in 1753 at Ovingham in the Tyne valley a few miles east of Corbridge, established himself as one of our greatest wood-engravers with his book, *History of Quadrupeds, 1790*, quickly followed by his *History of British Birds* (1797–1804), in which the figures are presented with astonishing accuracy, within powerful and decorative compositions in black and white.

Before looking at present landscapes it is necessary to touch on their natural post-glacial vegetation, even though relatively little work has been carried out on this, or on the stages where it has been altered by man. There are few, if any, areas where a 'natural' vegetation still survives, but least changes have probably occurred on the thin soils and exposed slopes of the highest land, on the Cheviot, the Pennines, and the Fell Sandstones and Whin Sill cuestas. Knowledge of changes that have occurred comes from studies of fossil pollen contained in peat bogs. By analysing the composition of pollen extracted by a core from various levels of a bog it is possible to work out the vegetational history of the area surrounding it. Throughout the Northumbrian uplands this analysis suggests that the earliest human clearances of woodland occurred relatively late, probably after 2000BC. Until then much of the area, probably up to about 2,000ft (610m), was covered by woodland, Scots pine and birch at the higher levels, with alder woods on poorly drained soils, and oak, hazel, rowan, elm and ash where the land was drier. A spell of wetter and warmer climate between 5000–3000BC probably initiated the reduction of forest cover, with the subsequent development and spread of peat on wet moorlands. Man's activities depleted woodland in the drier areas, and it seems likely that there was renewed and almost continuous deforestation from about AD500 onwards, not only through human settlement but also as a result of grazing of seedlings by stock which prevented regeneration. This grazing also helped the growth of grass at the expense of other plants, or, with woodland on poorer soils, favoured the development of heather moor. Additionally, sheep-grazing by monastic and lay landowners in medieval times, and on an increasing scale in the more peaceable conditions following the Union of Crowns in 1603, probably denuded the hills, especially the Cheviots, of their woodland cover. However, modified fragments of relict woodland do survive, mainly on steep, burnside slopes of the uplands. But most of the old forest has been replaced by heather moorland or new forest in the hills, and by farmland at lower levels.

The uplands can be divided into a number of landscape zones, each having a natural and/or man-made beauty, each providing its range of

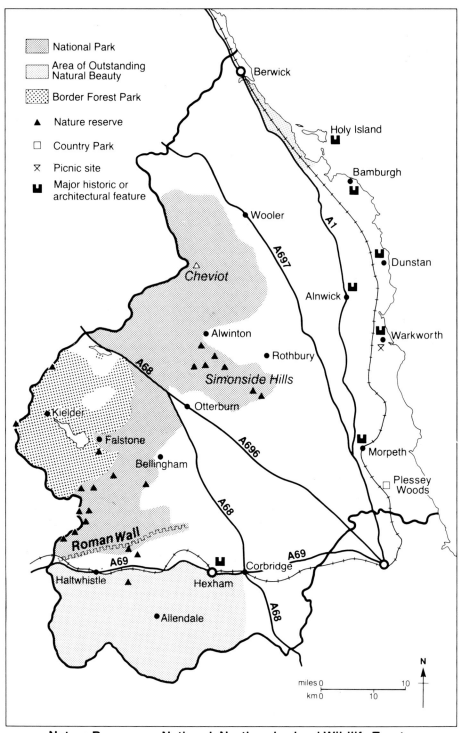

**Nature Reserves – National, Northumberland Wildlife Trust, Forestry Commission**

wildlife habitats, each contributing to the rich diversity of the area. It is this natural beauty, the wealth of flora and fauna, of geological and physiographic features, which, within the National Park area the Park Committee has a statutory duty to preserve and enhance. Outside the Park area, much of the upland country of the South Tyne and Allen watersheds now comes within the recently-designated North Pennines Area of Outstanding Natural Beauty (AONB). This recognises that it is of such fine landscape quality that there is a national and local interest in promoting conservation, encouraging visitors, but opposing unsuitable development.

## The Cheviot Hills

This zone is probably the most distinctive, both geologically and physically, within the National Park, formed wholly from igneous rocks – andesite lavas, volcanic ashes and tuffs, and a smaller capping of granite. Except for the too-many, too-regimented blocks of forestry plantations the hills are for the most part bare, windswept and grass-covered, this giving way at higher levels to a peat vegetation with heather, above the granite core. It is on Cheviot itself that there is an approach to an 'arctic-alpine' flora, seen only by the observant walker who appreciates these high and lonely places. The rocky ravines on the north-facing slopes by Auchope Cairn provide suitable habitats for mountain plants such as alpine scurvy grass, chickweed willow-herb, alpine willow-herb, rose-root, hairy stonecrop, mossy and starry saxifrages, together with bog whortleberry, alpine club moss, various bryophites and lichens.

On the summit plateaux and ridges of the central Cheviots high rainfall coupled with slow run-off has produced the acid, anaerobic conditions favouring the growth of peat. Above about 2,300ft (700m), on Auchope, Hedgehope and the central mass of Cheviot itself peat has accumulated to a depth of up to 10ft (3m), forming what is called blanket bog. This supports a vegetation comprised mainly of sedges, dwarf shrubs and bog mosses, while cotton grass is visually dominant, with both the common and hare's tail species present. Where peat has dried out, heather usually dominates, often associated with cloudberry, cross-leaved heath and the sphagnum mosses which are the main peat-forming plants in blanket bogs.

Below the granite core, as the slopes become steeper, accelerated rainwater run-off has eroded the blanket bog to produce gullies and peat-haggs. Between them, heather, cotton-grass and sedges dominate the fringes running down the hillsides until they meet the acidic grassland which dominates the slopes, ridges and plateaux below the highest tops. This grassland vegetation varies according to the soils, drainage and history of stock-grazing, but it is undoubtedly the feature which, in its greenness, surprises so many visitors. With the exception of a few areas mainly to the north of the main Cheviot summit, the range of these hills lacks the ruggedness of the Lake District mountains and the dourness of the high Pennines, a province for fell-walkers rather than rock-climbers.

It is on the steeper, well-drained slopes where the extensive swards of common and velvet bents and sheep's fescue grow, so important for the grazing stock. Where, however, this grassland is overgrazed, particularly between 1,000 and 2,000ft (305-610m), moor mat-grass (*Nardus stricta*) takes over, and it is communities of this which, from the late summer onwards, form such a distinctive feature of the hills, its withered leaves presenting so bleached an appearance. Coarse and unpalatable, it is not favoured by sheep, and in any case it has a low nutritional value. In wetter places, purple moor-grass (*Molinea caerulea*) tends to replace *Nardus*, often in company with bog-myrtle, bog moss and deer sedge. The drier soils support a richer and more colourful flora that includes tormentil, heath bedstraw, heath milkwort, bilberry and woodrush.

On many slopes up to as high as 1,000ft (305m), bracken is prolific. Since the deep rhizome of this invading plant needs at least 9in (20cm) of soil depth its presence could indicate evidence of former ploughing, and the fact that it flourishes so widely is often the result of hill-grazing by sheep rather than cattle, whose heavier tread destroys young bracken, thus preventing its growth and spread. Bracken is certainly abundant on the lower hill slopes where glacial drift has produced deep, clayey soils, and once established it can be eradicated only by regular cutting and crushing, arduous and time-consuming processes. Its one redeeming feature is probably the golden, russet colour it assumes from September onwards, retaining it, albeit in a duller and muted tone, throughout the winter, until new fronds rapidly green it again from late May onwards. During the months of high summer, particularly July and August, its dull green carpet blankets huge areas of the lower slopes, hides sheep (and adders), supports millions of flies and other insects, and, when wet, can turn a summer's walk into an unpleasant trial.

Although rock outcrops are rare, where they do occur extensive areas of scree are formed on steep slopes beneath them, as at Dunsdale, north of the Cheviot, and at Ingram Glidders. Such places, though freely drained, are harsh habitats for any plant but mosses which colonise the spaces between stones and provide sufficient foothold for various ferns to establish themselves. On the more stable rock ledges above the scree bilberry, harebell, wood sage, golden rod and greater woodrush are relatively common, adding colour and softness to these austere places.

It is on the bare Cheviot summit plateaux and ridges that you may expect to see and hear ravens, and, if you are lucky, a peregrine falcon, a species which seems to have increased in numbers in recent years. Numbers and species are more on the grassy hillsides, where bird life is characteristic of most upland country. Again, it is the birds of prey which are individually often most apparent, with buzzards, kestrels and sparrow-hawks quite common, the last-named showing a preference for small conifer plantations for nest sites. Although merlins are less numerous they do appear to be widespread over much of the open Cheviot country, and the same can be said of the short-eared owls.

No sound is more evocative of the wild, treeless uplands than the curlew's bubbling call heralding the late-arriving northern spring, by far the most melodic accompaniment to a walker's exploration of the high hill country. Appropriately it was selected as the symbol of the Northumberland National Park, gracing all the roadside indicators which advise motorists they have entered Park territory. Like many of the upland birds it is a migrant, nesting, like the lapwing, on the hills, summering there, but moving down to lowland areas and the coast in the autumn. Cuckoos, too, can be regularly heard in the hill country, though when seen they are frequently mistaken for birds of prey. Unusually, it is one of the smallest birds, the meadow-pipit, that probably has the widest habitat range, extending from the rough grazings at the lower levels to the high fells themselves, and it is meadow-pipits' nests which cuckoos seem to favour for laying their eggs. Stonechats, wheatears and skylarks are widespread on the open hills and valley sides; swallows and swifts swoop over the summer uplands far from their nesting-sites in and around buildings, and it is always satisfying to see ring-ouzels, even though their distribution is distinctly local, reflecting their preference for nesting-sites in the rocky crevices of small outcrops rather than on the open hillsides, and usually staying above the 1,000ft (300m) level.

Of all the wild animals of Cheviot country it is the least seen but most unexpected which claims greatest attention. Although they originated as domestic stock, the wild goats of the Cheviots, having bred wild for several centuries, are now feral. They are extremely shy, preferring the highest slopes in summer, feeding on shoots of young heather, deer sedge or cotton-grass, and in winter returning to lower levels for their food. I cannot claim to have seen any goats, but I am sure there would be no problems of identification. The expert Northumberland naturalist, Henry Tegner describes them as either grey-blue in colour, or having 'a skewbald pattern of brown and dirty-white'.

Outcrops of andesite on the lowest hill slopes, on the sides of valleys and burns, have often weathered to yield rich brown soils having a high organic content, particularly where they have accumulated on rocky ledges. The resultant herb communities probably represent relict oak, birch or ash woodland, excellently seen around Alwinton, where bird-cherry and aspen also occur, and burnet-rose grows in abundance. Oak tends to be more common on drier soils, birch on the more acidic ones, with alder on the boulder clay and where drainage is poor. Characteristic plant communities associated with such deciduous woodland include bluebell, primrose, wood sorrel, golden saxifrage, wood cranesbill, woodruff, wood sage, dog's mercy, golden rod, valerian and many species of ferns. Where base-rich spring water, or water draining from above, creates more marshy areas, cuckoo-flowers, marsh marigolds, melancholy thistle, spotted orchid, purple orchid and the lovely grass of Parnassus supplement the florisitic riches. Within the woodlands the rather limited range of bird species includes wood warblers, redstarts, and occasionally woodpeckers.

Valley bottoms, with their richer glacial or alluvial soils, support fertile grasslands, now enclosed by stone walls or the cheap iniquitous wire fencing. Such fields represent the 'inbye' land, improved in recent years by reseeding with productive and nutritious mixtures including timothy, rye and cocksfoot grasses, together with red clover. These provide good pasture for spring lambing and autumn tupping (when rams, or 'tups', are put to ewes), and they also yield the silage or hay crop grown as winter feed. Older, unimproved fields managed in the traditional way for a hay crop, invariably are far more species-rich both in grasses and herbs, and, to the visitor, show far more colour in early and high summer prior to the mowing of the hay.

Enclosed farmland is prominent in the Breamish valley around Hartside and between Low and High Bleakhope. Gorse, a plant associated with disturbed ground and thus an indication of earlier activities by man, is prevalent in the lower, eastern part of the valley, providing accents of colour in spring, but now so dense in places that control by burning is necessary. The shrub is predominant in the College valley and is also a feature for most of the length of the valley bottom. The Coquet valley, too, has areas of gorse on lower slopes of its hillsides, and in the valley bottom.

The 'braiding' of streams, particularly in the College and Breamish valleys, producing dry gravel beds, has resulted in some interesting, if inhospitable, habitats. Plants find difficulty in establishing footholds among the rounded stones and boulders in the free-draining gravelly sites, but with the help of lichens and mosses building up some organic base for them, a few low plants have succeeded, including shepherd's cress, wild thyme, sheep sorrel and mouse-ear chickweed.

## The Fell Sandstone Moors

Fell Sandstones predominate in the landscape to the south and east of the Cheviot hills. Nowhere is this more apparent than in a journey from Rothbury up Coquetdale. To the south the cuesta sandstone crags, seen so often as a shadowed, serrated line etched against a bright sky, mark the north face of the escarpment of the Simonside Hills. Drive further up the valley, and beyond Holystone the rocky, angular topography ahead and to the south contrasts even more sharply with the rounded outlines of the grass-covered Cheviot lavas. Similarly, though seen at a greater distance, the traveller on the A697 experiences the moorland ethos north of the Alnwick–Rothbury crossroads, as the main road swings northwards across the Rimside Moors. From the Vale of Till, the Cheviots rise to the west, smooth and sinuous, while away to the east the inward-facing crags of the Fell Sandstone create an arresting skyline.

The Fell Sandstone weathers to form poor sandy soils, with their mineral content leached out, producing acid conditions on which a dry heather moorland has developed. On the Simonside Hills this reaches 1,443ft (440m) on Tosson Hill, while the nearby crests of Ravens Heugh and Simonside are not far short of this height. Above Harwood Forest and on the Harbottle Hills, heather moorland covers extensive areas of upland between 800-1,300ft (244-396m), matched by the Rimside Moors; but the moorlands east of the Till are slightly lower than this.

Much of this open moorland is rough grazing, and also managed as grouse moor. Unusually, it is not common land, but remains under private ownership. In early spring, when other food is scarce, sheep find rich nutrient from young heather, and to ensure a good supply of fresh growth sensible moor management is necessary. Old heather needs to be controlled by careful burning – too much, or over-liming or over-draining, affects the ecological balance, and mat-grass takes over, and this has little or no nutritional value. Bracken has invaded the heather in a number of places, below Harbottle Crags, below the main Simonside ridge, and along the small valley courses of many burns. Grazing by cattle helps to keep this in check. Grouse also like young heather shoots, while the older heather provides good shelter and nesting sites. Thus, shepherd and gamekeeper have to some extent similar aims in moor-management.

Purple moor grass flourishes where damp flushes occur in heather moorland, often associated with bog-myrtle, conspicuous in early summer, with catkins of orange or red which appear before the leaves so noted for their resinous fragrance when crushed. The usual heather-grassland plants, tormentil, milkwort and eyebright, add splashes of colour, but it is the purple-massing colour of flowering heather which crowns these Fell Sandstone landscapes for two or three weeks in high summer, conveniently timing its appearance to coincide with August's

*Oak trees in Holystone North Wood Nature Reserve*

holiday season. Sandstone outcrops themselves yield few plants of interest, although bell-heather and cowberry add colour to rocky ledges, while bracken among the boulders sometimes hides the delightful climbing fumitory.

Between the two main areas of the Harbottle Hills and the Simonside ridges, the valley of the Grasslees Burn is one of the best sites in the National Park area for surviving alder woodland formerly so common along the sides of rivers and burns. Much more relict woodland occurs in the Holystone Burn area to the south-west of the village. Indeed, the woodlands of Holystone Burn and North Wood nearby are Nature Reserves leased by the Northumberland Wildlife Trust from the Forestry Commission. Holystone Burn comprises a wide range of upland woodland and moorland vegetation, with native oak and birch woods on the valley floor, with juniper scrub above. North Wood is an old, but very good example of upland sessile oakwood of uncertain origin, with many trees twisted and multi-stemmed, indicative of former coppicing and the removal of better specimens. Birch, rowan and holly are also present. Waymarked walks from the Forestry Commission car-park at Campville provide the best and most informative access to these important Reserves with their rich diversity of vegetation and bird life characteristic of upland woods and moors.

A mile west of Harbottle is the Harbottle Crags Nature Reserve, 390 acres (176ha) of heather moor dominated by spectacular outcrops of Fell Sandstone, of which the huge Drake Stone is the most prominent feature. A roadside car-park (Forestry Commission) has an Information Centre, from which a footpath and nature trail leads on to the reserve, climbing up to the Drake Stone and Harbottle Lake beyond it. In addition to the heather moor, managed for grouse, there is bracken, bilberry, cowberry, crowberry, bell-heather, rushes and sedges, damp flushes with bog myrtle, and sphagnum bogs. Thus, within a small compass, are all the features of rock, vegetation, and trees which typify Fell Sandstone country. Across the Coquet, to the north, the green Cheviots rise smoothly to distant, higher skylines, while the Simonstone ridge to the east frowns down on the patterned fields of the Coquet valley. Few such easily-reached viewpoints offer such great scenic rewards.

The area to the south, round Elsdon, is a relatively open, treeless landscape with farmland interspersed with rough acid grassland and bent-fescue pasture. Some walls enclose many fields, following various Enclosure Awards from 1731, while hawthorn hedges add variety, and provide better wildlife habitats. Deciduous woodland near the village and scattered trees on rough pasture soften the austere outlines. On parts of the Simonside and Harbottle Hills conifer plantations form dark-massing blankets particularly prominent from the A696 and the B6342 roads.

Covering 15,570 acres (6,228ha) between them, of which less than one-third is within the National Park area, Rothbury and Harwood Forests are owned and managed by the Forestry Commission. A well-screened car-park has been established on the minor road above Great Tosson, and a number of waymarked walks of different lengths and difficulty have been created within Rothbury Forest and through it on to the Simonside ridge. Above the plantations the crags of Simonside command respect, their steep cliffs offering good scope for rock-climbers. Waymarked paths offer easier ways to the top of the ridge, whose 2-mile (3.2km) extent includes the separate summits of Dove Crag at the east, Simonside in the middle, and Ravens Heugh to its west, with Tosson Hill, the highest point of all, three-quarters of a mile (1.2km) south-west of Ravens Heugh. The ridge is the highest land in central Northumberland, a panoramic viewpoint from which it is claimed you can see the whole of the county's coast, although I prefer to gaze north-westwards, when westering sunlight floods across the Coquet valley, modelling the coloured, crumpled landscape, and purpling the distant Cheviots.

Scots pines are the commonest trees in the plantations below the northern face of the ridge, and they flourish on the dry, infertile soil. Around the car-park larch provides variety and adds colour. Harwood Forest, extending down the gentler southern slopes of the escarpment, reaching as far as the Elsdon–Morpeth road, is considerably larger, and is

*The Drake Stone (left) and other sandstone boulders on Harbottle Hills*

roughly divided fifty-fifty between Scots pine and spruce, with very few larch. Forest tracks, open to pedestrians, penetrate it, and one ancient route between Hepple and Fallowlees cuts across the forest from north-west to south-east.

The Northumberland Wildlife Trust leases from the Forestry Commission as a nature reserve about 3,000 acres (1,200ha) of Harwood Forest forming part of the National Trust's Wallington estate. Although it has been planted since 1954 with Norway and Sitka spruce, and Scots and lodgepole pine, the reserve's main interests are its strips of semi-natural woodland, especially alder, and of marsh along the streams. Access to the Redpath and Fallowlees Reserve is by a forestry road from Harwood village, and parking is available at Redpath farm in the Reserve. Roe deer are abundant in this part of Harwood Forest, and the varied bird life includes black grouse.

Rothley Lake, adjoining the B6342 north of Rothley crossroads, also part of the Wallington estate, is another Northumberland Wildlife Trust Reserve, with access restricted to members of this, or other Conservation Trusts. There is no general public access. Rothley Lakes were created by Capability Brown for Sir Walter Blackett in the mid-eighteenth century, and occupy a glacial meltwater channel. The plantation, together with the nearby follies, are contemporary, and over the years the mixed woodlands and their associated wildlife have been managed very much with amenity and conservation in mind.

The Military Ranges occupy an area of relatively uniform country between the Harbottle Hills and Redesdale, characterised by gently rolling moorland at about 1,000ft (305m), above glacial deposits of boulder clay. Stewartshields, one of the earliest large-scale forestry plantations, lies within the area of the Military Ranges, a large, prominent block on the moors north-east of Rochester. A number of burns and small rivers have cut small valleys into the area, the most western of these, the Cottonshope Burn, being the most visually distinctive. A forestry track from the A68, at the Cottonshope Burn Picnic Area, leads northwards on to open moor on the western side of the valley, gradually swinging in north-eastwards to join Gamel's Path in about 4 miles (6.4km).

## Redesdale and North Tyne

Between the River Rede and the North Tyne, both of which rise very close to the Scottish Border several lonely, soggy miles apart, this mainly moorland zone developed on a succession of sandstones within the Carboniferous Limestone Group, and is deeply overlain by glacial deposits of boulder clay. Like the Military Zone, 1,000ft (305m) is an average height. However, both rivers have eroded deeper valleys into the softer, more shaley rocks of the Scremerston Coals, resulting in their valley land being much more fertile. Compared with the moors they are also sheltered, allowing farming to develop, with consequent enclosure of land in the eighteenth and nineteenth centuries.

Redesdale tends to be broad, open and fairly straight, contrasting with the upper part of the North Tyne below Falstone, which is narrower, more winding, and often more heavily wooded. Above Falstone, the Kielder Reservoir has brought a new element to the heavily afforested landscape. The central moorlands between the valleys, extending northwards from Bellingham for a dozen miles, and embracing Hareshaw Common, Corsenside Common, Thorneyburn Common, Troughend Common, Blackburn Common and Blakehope Fell, is predominantly heather moor, managed for grouse. At its northern and southern margins it shows a transitional character between heather and grass moor. Lonely roads running westwards from the A68 between West Woodburn and Blakehope reveal the spaciousness of these uplands, though they reach altitudes which are modest compared with those of Pennine country above Allendale and the South Tyne. In its course northwards from Bellingham the Pennine Way, too, recaptures its essential sense of wilderness walking after many miles in the gloom of Wark Forest.

Motorists wishing to sample a short stretch of this part of the Pennine Way may well enjoy the incentive given by the conspicuous cairn on Padon Hill, 820928, a mile (1.6km) north of the minor road from Dunn's Houses to Gatehouse and Greenhaugh. This well-built 'pepper-pot' is actually a monument to one Alexander Padon, although its inscription is now illegible. Padon Hill is, incidentally, at 1,240ft (389m), the highest point on the Way between Cross Fell and the Cheviots, whose long skyline in the distance must spur many way-farers with the realisation that, if the end is not visibly nigh, it is within attainable distance.

These moorland landscapes, with long low horizons, are rarely stimulating. Indeed, they are to say the least dreary, particularly in grey conditions. Perhaps afforestation is an improvement, and afforestation there certainly is, northwards in Redesdale, south and west to Kielder. The Forest Drive between Kielder and Byrness, is the easiest way by which to experience the open and the planted landscapes. This 12-mile (19km) forest road (toll payable) takes you through the developing Border spruce forests which give way at the highest point of the route, Blakehope Nick, 1,543ft (410m) to a short stretch of open moor with wide views northwards over Kielderhead Moor to the crest of the Cheviots. In addition to those at each end of the Forest Drive, numerous parking places along it are chosen to illustrate particular features of the forest's landscape and history.

Kielderhead Moor itself, covering over 2,000 acres (800ha) is a Northumberland Wildlife Trust Nature Reserve, with access only to members of a County Wildlife Trust, and then with a special permit. High altitude moorland includes the summits of Peel Fell and Carter Fell, the Border fence forming the Reserve's northern boundary. In spite of this all being wilderness country it has a remarkable habitat diversity. Scots pine, birch and willow scrub are present, especially in the cleughs; on the plateaux, apart from the high-level moorland, blanket bogs are of major interest, while a herd of feral goats is well-established.

### Wark and Irthing

Between the North Tyne valley and the Roman Wall the country is very largely coniferous forest, with Kielder Forest and Wark Forest covering vast areas of boulder clay moorland. Spruce and Scots pine, roughly in the ratio of seven to one, planted over the past fifty years, form an almost continuous blanket. A few small areas of moorland with craggy outcrops are unplanted, as are the smaller areas of bog, also recognised on the 1:50,000 OS map as white patches. From the natural history point of view these are particularly important, although their nature and remoteness are such that few visitors are likely to see them.

Five sites of major national importance, all SSSIs, and known collectively as the Irthinghead Mires, are Nature Reserves leased from the Forestry Commission. Coom Rigg Moss is the only National Nature Reserve within the National Park area, while Haining Head Moss, Hummel Knowe Moss, and Felicia Moss are Northumberland Wildlife Trust Reserves, and Butterburn Flow is across the Cumbrian boundary. They all lie within a 2½ mile (4km) radius, in a variety of topographical altitudes between 750 and 1,000ft (230-305m), and exemplify a range of vegetation.

Coom Rigg Moss, 690795, is a raised and blanket bog covering 88 acres (35.5ha), with heather, bog-moss, cross-leaved heath dominant, and hare's-tail cotton-grass common. Sphagnum dominates Haining Head Moss, 715750, which is similar in size, but this Moss is much richer floristically, with many typical bog species resulting from its wetter structure. Hummel Knowe Moss, 704714, covering 150 acres (61ha), is at a lower level than Haining Head, but is less rich in its bog vegetation, and Felicia Moss, 721775, of 105 acres (42ha), has an unusually undulating surface, full of small hummocks and hollows on a plateau at 1,000ft (305m). Heather on the humps, sphagnum in the hollows also form the surface pattern of vegetation at Gowany Knowe Moss, 730788, 48 acres (19ha), but with its higher water-table this is less rich in its bog flowers. Associated with these Irthinghead Mires is a smaller Reserve, The Lakes (NWT), a basin mire, very wet in places with a long soakaway at its eastern end with a variety of marsh and fen species. In its wetter parts the usual sphagnum bog species include sundew, cranberry and bog rosemary, with crowberry at the drier western end, and purple moor grass. Access to this Reserve, 740773, and all the others is by written permit.

### Roman Wall Area

This, the most-visited part of the National Park, is not only an historical landscape but also embraces a great variety of habitats. Characterised by the wave-like ridges of sandstone and the Whin Sill cuesta, between which are ice-gouged basins once filled with a myriad of small lakes but now covered with deep peat with only three stretches of open water remaining, the zone includes important geological exposures, rough moorland, grass moorland, improved pasture, peat mosses and isolated coniferous or mixed plantations.

The quartz dolerite of the Whin Sill weathers to form an easily-leached soil, so that on its long, southern dip-slope *Nardus* grassland is well-established, but on the ledges of the north-facing outcrop, together with the stabilised screes below, heather and bilberry abound, cowberry is abundant and rosebay willow-herb common. On limestone exposures beneath the dolerite rock rose adds small splashes of colour, and wild chives grow on the crags at Walltown.

It is the 'loughs' which add special distinction to the natural landscape of this area, and Crag Lough is many people's favourite, so prominent in the view from the Roman Wall between Peel and Hotbank Crags and lying beneath the frowning dolerite cliffs of the Whin Sill. Shallow, like its near neighbours Greenlee and Broomlee Loughs, it has gradually decreased in size through continual deposition of organic matter which accumulates to above water level. The plant succession associated with this starts with open water communities, passes through the intermediate stages of reed swamp and fen, and ends with willow carr or raised bog, probably colonised by certain species of sphagnum. The willow carr which has formed on the drier fen is a special feature of these Roman Wall loughs and includes sallow, bay and tea-leaved willow. The swamp at Crag Lough's western end is fed by alkaline water from the nearby limestone ridge, and has resulted in a great diversity of plant species. Crag Lough's bird life includes various water-fowl: mallards, tufted ducks, coots and swans.

Caw Lough, immediately south of Greenlee Lough, largest of the lakes, now has no open water, but is a basin mire fed by calcareous water, and shows an even richer vegetation in habitats ranging from 'poor fen' to rich fen meadow, while the carr woodland, dominated by sallow willow, contains many tall herbs such as meadow sweet.

South of the Wall, Grindon Lough, 806677, 3 miles (4.5km) north-west of Haydon Bridge, is a Northumberland Wildlife Trust Nature Reserve covering 22 acres (9ha), and can easily be viewed from the Stanegate which passes immediately to its south. It is particularly important for wintering waterfowl, and is noted for various geese – greylag, bean, and pink-footed – as well as for whooper swans, teal, widgeon and shovellers. The lough is too shallow for any of the diving duck.

### South of the Tyne Gap

Although the upper part of the South Tyne and the valleys of East and West Allen are markedly Pennine in character, the lower stretches have far more deciduous woodland than anywhere within this survey. Landscapes are softened by shelter-belts of trees and hedgerows, while the Allen gorge, below Cupola Bridge, 800592, on the A686 is one of Northumberland's most remarkable landscapes. The river follows a tortuous course between wooded banks 250ft (76m) high northwards to the Tyne, and for much of the way can be explored on foot, either from the south, at the site of Staward station near the Allendale lane end, or from the north, near where the Allen joins the Tyne, 799630. Most of this northern part of Allen Banks is National Trust property, with a variety of walks. Plankey Mill, roughly midway between north and south approaches, can also be reached by a minor road, and there is a footbridge over the Allen here.

Beech woodland and coniferous woodland with rhododendrons, contrast with a few small open riverside meadows, gay with mountain pansies in June, and wild garlic abounds. Oak, birch, ash, elder, hawthorn and the rarer juniper add to the woodland riches, and the Northumberland Wildlife Trust has recognised that the deciduous trees in part of the Allen gorge represent one of the best surviving fragments of ancient woodland in the county. Briarswood Banks, almost opposite Plankey Mill, is a 29 acre (12ha) Nature Reserve, with woodland paths through this rich relict woodland of ash, elm, oak, alder, hazel, birch, rowan, hawthorn, honeysuckle, holly and bird cherry. The ground layer is equally rich in species, and the presence of mosses and liverworts rare in the eastern half of England indicates that this woodland has never been cleared. Be warned, woodland walking in the Allen gorge can be very muddy and very slippery, so be shod accordingly!

Recently the Woodland Trust, with help from the Countryside Commission and local authorities, has bought two deciduous woodlands south of Hexham. Thirty-three acres (13ha) of Letah Wood, Newbiggin, in the lower valley of the Dipton Burn, contains splendid beeches, areas of wet alder woodland, and a pond, but is particularly noted for its April display of wild daffodils. To the south, near Ordley in the valley of the Devil's Water, Nunsbrough Wood has more variety of habitat, with water, riverbank, grassland, scrub and woodland, together with a network of public footpaths through its 41 acres (16ha). Both woodlands are to be managed to conserve and enhance their wildlife and amenity value, with footpath networks improved and extended.

Coniferous plantations cover about 20 per cent of the area of the National Park, over double that existing when the Park was designated in 1956. Additionally, and adjoining the western boundary of the Park, a large part of the Border Forest Park, designated concurrently with the National Park, lies on the English side of the Border, mainly in Northumberland, the whole now representing about 230 square miles (60,000ha) of dark green woodland. The traveller driving northwards along the A68 towards Carter Bar becomes aware of the extent of this blanket coverage of the Border hills to the west of the road beyond Rochester, and within another few miles the plantations have converged on the road, enveloping it until Catcleugh Reservoir is reached. Across the Border and west of Carter Bar Wauchope Forest clothes the Scottish side of the Cheviots. But it is on the once-bare uplands above the North Tyne where the greatest continuous areas of conifer plantations display most dramatically the man-made landscapes created during the past two generations.

The Forestry Commission was formed in 1919, with the main

objective of creating in the shortest possible time a 'strategic reserve' of timber against future emergencies. Today, 'economic' replaces 'strategic' in this objective, but the Forestry Commission's aims have considerably widened in scope and can be conveniently summarised:

1. To develop forestry and increase the production of wood for existing industries and those yet to be established by the extension and improvement of the forest estate.
2. To protect and enhance the environment.
3. To provide recreational facilities.
4. To stimulate and support the local economy of areas of depopulation by the development of forests, including new plantation and wood-using industry.
5. To further the integration of forestry and agriculture and to manage the estate as profitably as possible.

In the early 1920s the Commission was able to buy land at bargain prices. Two thousand acres (800ha) at Smales Farm near Falstone were bought in 1924, with planting starting two years later. In 1932, 47,000 acres (19,000ha), of what is now the nucleus of Kielder Forest were bought from the Duke of Northumberland, and those early years were a period of experiment and hope, with new plantations being laid out scientifically, usually in compartments of 25 acres (10ha) bordered by rides and firebreaks. Initially, tree-planting itself was by trial-and-error. It was soon found that putting young trees directly into peaty soil was not very satisfactory, but if drainage channels were cut and the young trees planted on to the turf ridges between them, much better results were obtained since the young tree roots are at the original soil level, above the damp layers of oxygen-deficient peat. Rotting plant roots in the upturned turf nourish the young tree roots until they spread outwards and downwards and are strong enough to cope with the difficult soil. The furrows act as drainage channels, thus reducing surface waterlogging, while the drier turf ridges prevent the young trees being smothered by weed growth during their early stages.

The success of this new method of planting was established by the time of the Kielder acquisition, thus opening the way for the development of new forests. The idea was not new for when John Hodgson visited the North Tyne in 1814 he commented that the land only needed draining and liming to make it suitable for growing trees, although he doubtless envisaged traditional hardwoods.

Planting made gradual progress during the 1930s and during World War II, but by far the greatest amount has been planted since then, especially in the 1950s. Lord Robinson, Chairman of the Forestry Commission from 1932 to 1952, and who had seen the first trees planted at Smales in 1926, returned in 1948 to fell the first thinnings there. Four years later, his ashes were scattered among the trees he loved, and he is commemorated not only by the living trees of Kielder Forest, but by a stone cairn at Whickhope, *677817*, in its very heart.

Following the realisation that Britain's timber needs were greater now than ever, post-war planting accelerated rapidly, and more and more land in the Border country was acquired. However, it soon became obvious that more people were going to be needed to provide the work-force. The nearest large towns were on Tyneside, at Hexham and Berwick, while the nearest villages at Bellingham, Otterburn, Wark and Wooler were some miles from the Forest, and any workers there would need transporting, a time-consuming and costly business. Seven special Forestry villages were built, of which three – Byrness, Kielder and Stonehaugh – were in Northumberland. Kielder and Stonehaugh are within the Border Forest Park, and Byrness on the National Park/Forest Park boundary in Redesdale.

The town-planning consultant Dr Thomas Sharp designed the new villages, including the houses, facilities for social life, shops and schools. Although the white-washed houses are distinctive and serviceable, they bear little if any relationship to local building styles, and still resemble vaguely urban groups in forest and moorland settings. Undoubtedly their new occupants took some time to settle in, particularly as many came from industrial backgrounds. A few stayed only briefly but most remained so that these artificially-planted communities in one of the most isolated areas in England eventually took root.

Land continued to be acquired until 1969, and today planting is almost complete. It seems unlikely that expansion will continue on a similar scale in the future, and, as older plantations reach maturity and are felled it is expected that by the early 1990s re-afforestation will represent the greater proportion of the annual planting programme. However, lessons have been learned, and if replanting followed the same pattern as the original planting it would merely perpetuate the uniformity of shape and colour which has produced so much criticism of the Forestry Commission's past endeavours.

Almost 300 sq miles (777 sq km) of land has been acquired for forestry in the Border Forest Park. Boundaries and names of individual forests have changed. Four blocks of forest in Tynedale and Redesdale – Kielder, Falstone, Redesdale and Wark, form a continuous sweep now known as Kielder Forest, extending over almost 100,000 acres (40,000ha). With such enormous areas to prepare for planting mechanical methods of preparation have necessarily replaced the old manual ones. Many types of tractor-hauled ploughs have been used, all producing furrows separated by long ribbons of turf between, about 5ft (1.5m) apart. Young trees, raised from seed in the Forestry Commission's own nurseries, are transplanted when they are two to four years old in their final positions on the prepared ridges: either in circular holes cut with a semi-circular spade like a bulb-planter, or in spade-cut slits in the turf, at a five-foot spacing each way. One thousand five hundred young trees are needed for each acre (0.4ha), allowing for the spacing of rides and fire-breaks. This represents a day's work for a trained forester. A planting programme of 1,000 acres (400ha) a year required 1½ million young trees and the principal nursery at Widehaugh, 2 miles (3.2km) east of Hexham, raises about 7 million trees each year.

Five species of conifers account for almost all the afforestation of the past fifty years in the Border Forest Park, mainly spruces, easy to establish and capable of giving high yields on peaty soils in areas of moderately high rainfall. On lower, more fertile and better-drained land Norway spruce is preferred. This is the familiar Christmas tree, which not only thrives in reasonably sheltered conditions but can also withstand the hard valley frosts common in spring. On higher slopes Sitka spruce from the coastal area of British Columbia and Alaska is more suitable, being more resistant to wind and capable of withstanding exposure and poorer soil conditions.

On heathery, drier ground neither of these species grows well in their early stages, and pines are usually planted – the native Scots pine on drier knolls, and the hardier but similar Lodgepole pine, mainly from Washington or British Columbia, on deeper peat areas that nevertheless sustained a good growth of heather. In areas where bracken grew among the original vegetation, thus indicating well-drained soils, Japanese larch thrives – easily recognisable by its light-green spring and early summer colouring, and its bare russet twigs of autumn and winter. Young larches have an additional advantage in that they do not readily burn, and also suppress inflammable growth beneath them, so are useful as being live fire-breaks.

Biological maturity of conifer plantations may take from sixty to eighty years, but in terms of economics, the average tree maturity in the Border Forest Park is more likely to be forty-five years. However, around twenty years after planting, young trees are beginning to crowd each other so that thinning becomes essential if the best trees are to develop successfully. In this operation about one tree in five is felled, after first 'brashing' some or all of the trees in a plantation – a pruning operation which removes all the side branches up to a height of 5 or 6ft (1.5-1.8m), thus improving access, reducing fire risk and helping the formation of better timber with fewer knots.

After felling trees marked for thinning, and trimming away the remaining branches, foresters haul the resultant logs to the side of a forest road for transport to sawmills or other consumers. The forest harvest of either thinnings or mature timber is mainly pulpwood and logs. Pulpwood goes to make paper, packaging or reconstituted wood such as chipboard, while logs go for general construction timber, planks, pallets and packaging. These may seem unglamorous, prosaic end-products for many years of hard endeavour and much patience, but they are important ingredients of our national economy. Wood is our one natural resource which is renewable, and the estimated half-million tons of sustained annual timber harvest from the Border Forest Park help us to see the coniferous landscapes in a different perspective.

Attitudes to thinning have changed as experience and research have shown that where this was done selectively in plantations on higher land, the disturbance made the remaining trees in a stand more vulnerable to high winds and many were blown down. By the mid-1960s, almost all thinning was limited to trees at lower levels, although clear felling of the Sitka plantations was carried out. It is now realised that thinning plantations standing above 820ft (250m) is not acceptable. As this embraces about 85 per cent of the whole of Kielder Forest the resultant harvest will be one of smaller trees than originally envisaged, but the losses are likely to be offset by unexpected gains, as labour-intensive operations like brashing are abandoned and a more mechanised felling of mature trees is easier, involving a lower workforce.

The bigger, more sophisticated and efficient machines used today need more operating space and good forestry roads to move along. The provision of forest roads was recognised from the outset as a priority, and although some were created in the 1930s the post-war decades saw a massive road-building programme carried out, still continuing today, so that in Kielder Forest alone over 500 miles (800km) of forest roads have been constructed. Most are private roads used only by Forestry Commission vehicles, but one road, linking Kielder Castle with Byrness in Redesdale, has been improved to take visitors' cars, and provides – on payment of a toll – not only a useful short cut between these two places, but a rewarding experience through a series of views of the high ground of Fell Sandstone country, its open and afforested landscapes, and, if you are lucky, some of its wildlife.

Kielder Castle itself, completed in 1775 as a shooting-lodge for the Duke of Northumberland, and used regularly through a succession of autumns during grouse and blackcock shooting, has become the administrative centre of the Forestry Commission within the Forest Park. It has also been developed as a Visitor Centre, with interpretative displays, information rooms, toilets, car parks, a shop and tea-room, while nearby are a picnic site, forest trails, waymarked walks and a nature reserve.

The Forestry Commission has other extensive forests partly or wholly within the National Park. Wark Forest, within the Kielder block, represents 13.5 per cent of the Park area, while others in Redesdale, at Rothbury, Harwood, Kidland and Chillingham, together add on half as much again, so that over one fifth of the National Park is afforested by state forests. South of the Tyne valley, Slaley Forest is the main forest area, covering 3,000 acres (1,200ha) of gritstone moorland plateau between the Derwent valley and the Devil's Water.

Afforestation of any kind produces significant effects on the landscape, and opinions vary as to whether coniferous plantations enhance or detract from landscape beauty, opinions often influenced by the size and shape of plantations. Since large-scale planting has been going on for over fifty years, fewer people remember these landscapes from pre-planting days. But Forestry Commission plantations on the Cheviot Hills have a more recent history. About 11,000 acres (4,500ha) of land in the Cheviot area is now under commercial forestry, two-thirds of this Forestry Commission, one-third in private or company ownership.

Most of Kidland Forest in upper Coquetdale was planted between 1950 and 1970, while the small plantations at Uswayford, 890170, and Threestoneburn, 960200, were added in the mid-1970s. As the National Park was designated in 1955, there has been a clash of interests. The Park Authority are responsible 'for the preservation and enhancement of natural beauty, and the public's enjoyment of the Park'. It is arguable whether the Cheviot plantations have added to the beauty of the clean lines of the Cheviot's wilderness landscapes, while public access and enjoyment have not been markedly enhanced. The Park Authority also has a statutory duty to the needs of the primary land use, agriculture and forestry, and these, unfortunately, are exempt from planning control. Although trees may be considered an agricultural crop, they differ from most crops in having a very long production cycle, offering no scope for annual or biennial correction. Once a plantation is decided upon and the ground prepared, at least thirty years elapse before any harvest may be gained. Even after that time, the monocultural use of rough grazing for timber production ensures that the land cannot easily be used for anything else, as the thin topsoil will have been exhausted, with conifer needles providing very little usable compost. Some fertilisation will allow for reafforestation, thus perpetuating plantations in selected landscapes.

The Forestry Commission, largely through ignorance, in their planting programmes and methods between the wars, did not endear themselves to the public. The 1950s were not much better, but in the past two decades a more enlightened approach, helped by the advice from landscape consultants, has improved the Commission's public image. Plantations in the Cheviots, visually producing less of a blanket coverage than in the huge expanses of Kielder and Redesdale, illustrate good and bad points of afforestation.

Near Trowupburn, 876265, above the College valley, straight-edged plantations are particularly unsympathetic to the landscape along the slopes of Loft Hill. Skyline planting here, and above Fairhaugh, 875123,

*Kidland Forest, above Coquetdale*

above the Usway Burn, ruins the smooth contours of Cheviot uplands. Above Elsdonburn, 862293, near Kilham, the eastern hillside of a lovely, lonely valley has been ruined by straight-edged plantations dissected by arrow-straight rides and firebreaks producing precisely the type of afforested landscape so rightly condemned many years ago.

On the credit side, however, co-operation between the National Park Authority, the Forestry Commission and private forestry interests, with the inevitable compromises on all sides, has brought about improvements and changes in forestry practices. Some firebreaks, originally let for grazing, which proved expensive in terms of fencing and inefficient in practice are being planted up. Felling programmes are given much more careful thought, with allowances made for them to be modified on the ground to conform to landscape features and contours. Much greater attention is being paid to planting lines, particularly along roads and walks such as Clennell Street in Kidland Forest. Skyline planting is to be reduced, as between Dunmoor Hill and Cunyan Crags above Threestoneburn. Improvements along plantation boundaries, by the increased use of hardwoods, is important, particularly where these adjoin main roads and public rights-of-way. Blocks of larch add seasonal colour to the predominantly spruce and pine plantations on Freddon Hill,

955270, west of Wooler. Sensible mixed planting softens the dull monotony of vast areas of spruce, and adds to the visual amenity of some landscapes. Larch is particularly useful in this respect, as may be appreciated by A68 travellers driving through upper Redesdale in October when the larch needles are yellowing, making colourful contrasts with the dark green of spruce and pine.

Indeed, the importance of this A68 corridor through the National Park, between Elishaw and Carter Bar, has prompted the Forestry Commission to formulate an outline management plan for the landscape to ensure not only that the forest's attractive appearance is maintained, but that it continues increasingly to provide a good area for recreational activities. Two areas in the Rede valley have been singled out for management: an Area of Special Landscape Consideration covering about 3,530 acres (1,429ha) along the valley's broad area, and 1,775 acres (718ha) in the moderately-sheltered part of the lower valley. This Lower Valley Working Circle is to be managed with the aim of preserving the forest cover, with pleasant woodland surroundings for recreational facilities. Felling is to be small in scale, and forest tree species will provide necessary restocking, with more native broad-leaved trees established in small groups by the main road and along the burns.

In the larger area more attention is to be given to the timing and extent of forestry operations, to preserve the forest landscape at the same time as felling, clearing and restocking are taking place. Clearfelling will be restricted in both place and time so that outlooks from principal viewpoints will not reveal huge areas of mass devastation. An irregular pattern of felling will take regard of species; age and height will help towards this aim, and more attention will be given to the treatment of trees by public paths and walks.

# 8
# EXPLORING THE UPLANDS

When National Parks were designated over thirty years ago it was envisaged that those who used them most would be participants in active recreation – walking, climbing, cycling, canoeing, bird-watching etc. The motor-car explosion has changed the picture so that in most National Parks, and Northumberland's is no exception, sightseeing by car has become the accepted norm, although recent evidence suggests that an increased proportion of visitors now like to explore the Park on foot, even if they have arrived by car, a factor necessitated by the poor public transport situation. Undoubtedly, improvements in signposting and waymarking, as well as the maintenance in good order of a network of public footpaths and bridleways, encourage visitors to be more adventurous in their explorations. In this context, incidentally, the Northumberland National Park Authority is unique among all National Parks in being the responsible body for public footpaths and bridleways throughout the county and not just within the Park area. Their burgeoning list of useful publications on the subject, excellently written and illustrated, now embraces most popular parts of the National Park and is of great value to walkers in particular. A guided walks programme through the normal summer season, with many specialist walks then, and at other times of the year, is increasingly well supported. This chapter is concerned mainly with the motorist sightseer and the walker, while cyclists should also find plenty that is relevant.

## Motor Tours

A glance at an appropriate motoring map immediately illustrates the main problem facing motorists. Only one trunk road crosses the National Park area. A68 from Corbridge, joined by the A696 from Newcastle north of Otterburn, neatly bisects the Park in its course through Redesdale. Twenty miles to the east the A697 approaches the north-eastern edge of the Park at Wooler, while the A69 follows the South Tyne valley between the Park's southern boundary and the northern Pennines. One minor road, the B6320, accompanies the North Tyne to Bellingham, continuing as C200 past Kielder Water to provide a link across the Border into Liddesdale. Thus, most routes radiate like the skeleton of a fan from Tyneside; but within the National Park in general, and the Cheviot region in particular, lateral routes are either non-existent, or few and far between. Circular trips incorporating Cheviot country or the Border Forest Park necessarily involve Scottish sections, although that is no bad thing!

Away from the main roads, garages and petrol pumps are rare, especially in the upper valleys of Coquetdale, the North Tyne, and the Allendales. Roads are narrow and winding, with limited sight-lines. Verges are generally small, with few roadside parking places, although the A68 in particular is generously provided with these, notably in the Redesdale forest area. Some upland minor roads have unenclosed sections, where sheep grazing the moorland edge are the main hazard. It is quite remarkable how often they decide to cross the road in front of an approaching vehicle. Although farming is predominantly pastoral, so far as cattle are concerned this is more stock-rearing than dairying, so motorists are less likely to be frustrated by the twice-daily movement of milking cows as is the case in some National Parks.

The tours suggested vary in length from 30 to 100 miles (48-160km), but qualities of landscape, scenery, and buildings are the criteria, not mileage. Each is a circular tour starting and finishing at one or other of the more popular holiday centres, although obviously intervening or other starting-points can be used. Ordnance Survey Landranger Maps, Scale 1:50,000, are far more useful than smaller scale motoring maps.

*Auchope (right) with the Pennine Way and the ravine of Henhole*

### 1. Wooler – Whittingham – Thropton – Elsdon – Carter Bar – Morebattle – Wooler

(Whole day to do it justice)

This tour embraces the Cheviots' northern section, giving outstanding views throughout. Take the A697 south from Wooler, with a possible detour near Brandon, to the Breamish valley and National Park Information Centre at Ingram. Leave the A697 at Powburn for the minor road through Glanton to Whittingham, which is worth a stop to admire village setting, church, and former pele tower. South-west past Callaly Castle (open to public occasionally), Cartington, and descend to Coquet valley at Thropton. Detour to Rothbury if desired, or tour could start there. B6341 up Coquet valley, with superb views of Simonside Hills, to Hepple, across river past Harehaugh (picnic area) and up wooded valley of Grasslees Burn to Billsmoor viewpoint (parking area). Short moorland stretch to Elsdon, noting Mote Hills on east of road. Village merits exploration; green, church, pele-tower. B6341 to Otterburn, joining the A696 and heading northwards up Redesdale. Forests become prominent after joining A68. Good picnic places off road near Byrness. Continue past Catcleugh Reservoir, and long climb to Carter Bar. Pause at Border for quiet reflection and panoramic views into Scotland.

*Pasture in Grasslees Valley above Elsdon*

Long descent towards Jedburgh. Can leave A68 at Camptown for minor road to Oxnam, Crailinghall and Morebattle, or can continue into Jedburgh (beautiful abbey, historic buildings, good shops), taking A698 2 miles north of town. In both cases, turn off A698 for Eckford, and turn right, B6401, eastwards to Morebattle and Town Yetholm. Turn right here for Kirk Yetholm (nice cottages round green, end of Pennine Way), and follow Bowmont Water along northern foot of Cheviots, past Kilham, Kirknewton and Akeld to Wooler.

## 2. Rothbury – The Corn Road – Chollerford – Bellingham – Otterburn – Elsdon – Rothbury

If a visit to Wallington Hall (NT) is to be included, it is better to do this tour in the opposite direction, so as to be at Wallington in the afternoon, when the house is open. Route southwards from Rothbury crosses the rich heartlands of Northumberland, using the B6342 following the Corn Road turnpiked in 1753–4, with views over wooded parklands, arable and pasture, shelter-belts and plantations. Right-angled bends are numerous, and high, hump-backed bridge south of Wallington needs care. Go across A696 and A68, where the road becomes the A6079 and continues past Chollerton (church, farm-group), into the North Tyne valley. The village of Wall merits a small diversion before retracing route to Chollerford (diversion to Chesters Roman fort). Take the B6320 via Simonburn (diversion to village) and Wark to Bellingham.

Choose here between direct moorland route, B6320, over Hareshaw and Troughend Commons to Otterburn, or take longer route up North Tyne valley by unclassified road to Lanehead, Greenhaugh and Gatehouse with a diversion there (EH signs) to see Black Middens Bastle-House. Then turn north-east and take minor road across moors to A68, turning right and left to Otterburn, A696 and B6341 to Elsdon, and the Grasslees Burn road to Hepple and Rothbury (details as for Tour 1).

### 3. Bellingham – Kielder – Bonchester Bridge – Carter Bar – Byrness – Bellingham

This tour includes Kielder Water, Kielder Forest, a Scottish section, and Redesdale.

Take the C200 south of the river up the North Tyne valley to Kielder Water, for a visit to Tower Knowe viewpoint and Information Centre. Further car-parks and viewpoints occur along the road. Kielder Castle should be visited for its interpretative displays about forestry, and it is a short, easy walk to Kielder Viaduct from the Bakethin car-park near Kielder village. Continue north-westwards, crossing Border at Deadwater, and following unenclosed road down Liddesdale for 3 miles (4.8km) to Saughtree. Turn right (north) on B6357 for about 10 miles (16km) almost to Bonchester Bridge. Turn right (east) on A6088, joining A68 at Carter Bar, to appreciate the long descent to Catcleugh Reservoir and the forests of Redesdale. Continue past Rochester, keep on A68 at Elishaw, and turn right on B6320 for a return to Bellingham.

### 4. Hexham – Bellingham – Kielder – Byrness – Redesdale – Corbridge – Hexham

A tour incorporating moorland and valley scenery, the Forest Drive, industrial remains, a castle, a small historic town, and a Roman centre.

Take A6079 northwards from Hexham to Chollerford, with a small diversion at Wall to see an attractive village. Turn left beyond Wall on to B6320, crossing North Tyne at Chollerford, and heading for Bellingham and Kielder Water. At Kielder Castle turn north on to Forest Drive (toll) for a challenging, but not unduly rough, 12-mile (19km) drive through different types of forest landscapes. Leaflet, available at Kielder Castle, points out features of interest. Numerous small car-parks on the way.

Join A68 at Byrness in Redesdale, and follow main road southwards to the Portgate (roundabout) where it crosses B6318 and the line of the Roman Wall. Do not be in too much of a hurry. At Corsenside, 2 miles (3.2km) south of B6320 (Otterburn–Bellingham) crossroad, divert east

*Redesdale Artillery Ranges*

on a farm road to see Corsenside church (setting, architecture, monuments). Less than another mile south, notice re-erected Roman milestone by gate on west side of road. South of West Woodburn, beyond sharp bend, notice fortress-like ruin of engine-house of Ridsdale ironworks (c1840). All along this road repeated undulations carry it across the grain of the underlying strata.

One mile south of Portgate turn off A68, and follow EH signs for Aydon Castle. With a slight detour Halton Castle can also be seen. From Aydon, follows signs for Corbridge, entering town from north-east. It deserves a lengthy visit, and be sure to include the Tourist Information Centre in the Vicar's Pele. End with a visit to Corstopitum Roman settlement west of the town, before returning to Hexham.

### 5. Hexham – Langley – West Allendale – Alston – South Tyne Valley – Greenhead – Military Road – Hexham

A tour into the northern Pennine country, with softer woodland landscapes of two valleys, and the Military Road accompanying the Roman Wall as an historical climax.

Take B6305 west from Hexham, showing characteristic straightness of eighteenth-century enclosure road. Good views to north. Notice lead-smelting chimney at Stublick. At Carts Bog turn left on A686, descending to cross beautiful, wooded gorge of West Allen at Cupola Bridge, continuing southwards up West Allendale before climbing over moorland to Alston (Cumbria), a market town surrounded by high, wild fells of north Pennines. Cross South Tyne, keeping right, to take A689 northwards down valley. One mile past Slaggyford, keep right on unclassified road for Knarsdale, soon crossing river and climbing.

Widening views over valley; farms and hamlets built in Pennine traditional styles, with stone walls and roofs. Note Lambley Viaduct (disused) far below. Continue to Rowfoot, turning left to pass behind Featherstone Castle, where it is worth stopping for a riverside stroll through the park. Cross river at Bridge End, following signs for Greenhead. Short detour north to Thirlwall Castle forms a pleasant prologue to the journey eastwards along Military Road, B6318. Allow plenty of time for many stops and local explorations (a) to Cawfields Picnic Area, (b) to Steel Rigg car-park – both on the north side of road, (c) Once Brewed Car-park and Information Centre, south of road, (d) Housesteads, (e) at Brocolitia, and finally (f) at Chesters, from where it is not far back to Hexham.

### 6. Hexham – Allendale – Allenheads – Blanchland – Hexham

This tour incorporates valley, moorland, lead-mining survivals, interesting and varied villages, with a touch of forestry.

Take B6305 as for Tour 5, but on Stublick Hill, before reaching chimney, fork left onto B6304, joining B6303, for Allendale Town. Enjoy a short saunter round its wide wooded market place. Good local history and walks leaflets available in shop. Take B6296 southwards, following eastern side of East Allendale, with good views across valley to moorland landscapes. Notice, higher up valley, scattered farms, representing 'dual economy' small-holdings of lead miners. New woodlands soften the melancholy of vanished industry around Allenheads, and village is a small, sheltered oasis amid wild moors. Good pub, too.

Take unclassified road climbing east out of village. From top of hill look back to the lead-mining landscape of small reservoirs, water-courses and the remains of spoil heaps. Wild road over moors (County Durham) to head of Rookhope, and more mining remains and some new re-working of old spoil. Turn left (north) on unclassified road, crossing Hunstanworth Moor before descending into Derwent valley, with plantations and shelter-belts around Blanchland, on the Northumbrian bank of the river. As you admire the neat cottage terraces of grey-brown stone, give silent thanks to the Lord Crewe Trustees who rebuilt this village in 1750 for local lead-miners. Be thankful, too, that the old monastic layout has been preserved, and that other monastic buildings survive, and are used. B6306 north-eastwards from Blanchland is the route back to Hexham, giving good distant views of Derwent Reservoir before entering Slaley Forest and the edge of Dipton Wood and the descent to the Tyne valley.

## Walks

Although no OS Outdoor Leisure Maps on the 1:25,000 scale have yet been prepared for the Northumbrian Uplands, much of the area is covered by the OS Pathfinder Series at the same scale. Each sheet embraces a much smaller area, but is handier to use and includes all necessary details useful to walkers, including rights-of-way and field boundaries. Additionally, the National Park and Countryside Department publish excellent Guides which are models of clarity and include sections of 1:25,000 maps, as well as much local and natural history. Allendale Parish Council publishes a useful pack of walks leaflets.

While many paths are identified by signposts and yellow waymarks, and many bridleways have blue markers, many others lack such identification, mainly because some farmers and landowners have not given permission for waymarking. Thus, while you *know* you have a right to use a waymarked track, the absence of waymarking does *not* imply there is *no* right-of-way. If the OS map indicates a right-of-way, even though it may not be apparent on the ground, it does exist and you can use it. In so doing you should recognise that many public paths cross meadows and pastures where important hay crops are critical to the farming economy. It is therefore essential that in using paths which cross such fields you keep in single file to reduce unnecessary damage to mowing grass.

Gates should be left as you find them, which usually means closed. Wandering stock can become mixed with others, mate prematurely, upset cropping regimes, stray on to the roads or even cause a spread of infection. Courteous behaviour to farmers and landowners costs nothing; its rewards are for the people who follow you. The law now allows farmers to graze some breeds of beef bulls with cows or heifers in fields crossed by rights-of-way. It is advisable always to give them a wide berth and not to provoke them. Dairy bulls, usually black and white Friesians, should not be grazed where there are public paths, and in any case should be avoided. Young bullocks are invariably curious about humans and will frequently come towards you, but will do nothing more than that, unless provoked. If you walk with a dog, keep it under control, preferably visibly on a lead. This goes some way to reassuring farmers that you are a responsible and thoughtful person.

A similar attitude of common sense should apply to your clothing. It should be comfortable and practical, particularly so far as footwear is concerned. Walking boots are best, not climbing boots, which may be too heavy. Boots give protection to ankles, which can easily be sprained, especially in descending steep or rough slopes. 'Commando', 'Vibram', or 'Skywalk' soles help to give a good grip, especially on wet grass. Strong shoes or even 'trainers' are suitable for straightforward field or riverside paths, but not for fell-walking, and if you expect to be walking on the 'tops', a compass is advisable. It helps navigation in mist and low cloud, provided you know how to use it in conjunction with a map. But common sense is the best guide; if weather conditions are bad, or forecasts suggest they could become bad, there is little point in seeking trouble. Good, low-level walks abound.

Almost one-third of the 270 miles (434km) of Britain's first long-distance footpath, the Pennine Way, passes through Northumberland. The South Tyne valley section has fine river scenery, enfolded by the austere northern Pennines; from Thirlwall to Cuddy's Crags west of Housesteads, the Roman Wall section represents the historic climax of the whole route compensating for some of the dreary forest parts of the north. By far the longest and loneliest section of the Pennine Way is represented by the 18 miles (29km) along the Cheviot ridge, following the Border fence, from Chew Green to The Schil, beyond which the track crosses into Scotland for the last 5 miles (8km) downhill to Kirk Yetholm. Perhaps it is signficant that footpath erosion by walkers' boots is much less in the Northumberland part of the Pennine Way than in more trodden sections in Derbyshire and Yorkshire. I wonder why more walkers don't attempt the challenge in a southerly direction, thus getting the most gruelling miles done first.

### 1. Harthope Valley: Langlee – Housey Crag – Langleeford
### (4 miles-6.4km)

A short walk to a superb viewpoint on the best-known 'tor' in the Cheviots.

Leave the car on the grassy area by the road almost opposite the lonely Langlee cottage. Walk across the bridge and soon turn right off the farm track (sp Threestoneburn). Follow a grassy track above Harthope Burn, gradually gaining height across open pasture, with good views of the burn's braided, gorsey course. Aim for circular stell ahead, contouring to its right, across a small burn, and climb towards a boundary fence. Turn left by this, and climb steadily until you reach a gate. Go through this and cross open moorland, boggy in places, to Housey Crag, prominent in the view. Like all rocky outcrops it exerts a strong appeal, particularly in landscapes where outcrops are rare. Given clear weather (and the walk is not really worth doing otherwise), the rewards are great, with Hedgehope's shapely cone dominating the forward view, and Cheviot's bulky plateau across the upper valley. The view below shows typical land-use in a splendid Cheviot valley – heather and bracken slopes, relict deciduous woodland and planted shelter-belts, scree, improved and enclosed grassland, riverside haughs. Man and nature are here in harmony, and nothing displeases.

From the tor, descend north-eastwards to join the farm track that leads down to Langleeford amid its plantations. Cross the burn, turn right, and follow the valley road back to the car.

### 2. Old Bewick – Blawearie – Corbie Crags – Old Bewick
### (4 miles-6.4km)

Moorland walk in Fell Sandstone country, with superb panoramic views.

Park in hamlet of Old Bewick, but don't obstruct any farm entrances. Follow track past row of cottages, through a gate and up the steep hill ahead fringed with Scots pine. Old Bewick Hill on right is site of important Iron Age fort. The rough cobbled track continues through two more gates, with drystone wall on left. At third gate the vegetation changes from bracken and rough pasture to heather moorland. Fork right where track divides, aiming for sycamore trees ahead, and passing Bronze Age burial mound on left, together with cup-and-ring marked stones. Continue to ruins of Blawearie, abandoned for half a century amid its trees, and rhododendrons. Retrace for 40yd (36.6m) and follow direction arrow on yellow waymark amid bracken on left, near small stream. Follow path through bracken, over boggy area, to another waymark directing you to a cairn-marked track through heather. A white-topped guide post encourages you past another ancient encampment and a more modern pillbox to Corbie Crags. Continue generally southwards to the meeting of two streams aiming for a gate before which you turn right, away from the streams, keeping a fence on the left, and heading up the side of a small valley. Keep this on the left and follow a subsequent fence to a gate.

Choose here either for the easy way down the track to the road that leads back to Old Bewick, or, preferably, turn right along a rutted bridleway which climbs the eastern spur of Old Bewick Hill, keeping fence on left as far as a wicket gate in a drystone wall. Bear left and descend steeply, turning right below some rhododendrons, and contour westwards to a stile in the lane where you started.

### 3.  Alwinton – Clennell Street – Wholehope – Copper Snout – Shillmoor – Alwinton (8 miles-12.9km)

A long walk, along an ancient drove road, with a short forest stretch, some rough hill country, a couple of steep bits, and a concluding mile along a road. Exemplifies Cheviot landscapes and history.

Good car-park (NP) in Alwinton. Cross village green and footbridge over Hosedon Burn. Turn left on good track climbing steadily, relentlessly northwards. This is Clennell Street, a 12 mile (19km) track used formerly by reivers, pedlars, drovers and smugglers, between Cocklawfoot and Alwinton. You will appreciate the backwards view over Coquetdale more than they did. Clennell Hall shelters in woodlands to the east. Beyond the cottage of Clennellstreet on the right the track becomes grassy, eventually coming in sight of Kidland Forest. Swinging westwards it continues climbing steadily to the forlorn ruins of Wholehope, an abandoned shepherd's cottage, later a Youth Hostel.

Enter the forest, keep left at a junction of forest tracks and walk through this forest section (1/2 mile-805m). Soon after emerging, turn left at small cairn (waymarked) on to rough grassland, aiming for the plantation corner ahead. Keeping a fence on your left, go through a gate near a good stell on Saughy Hill, on to an improving grassy track climbing gently to Copper Snout, one of many rounded hills in the panoramic view. This is part of the 'dry training area' of the Otterburn Ranges, but there is no danger provided you keep to the path. A good track continues southwards to Shillmoor in the Coquet valley, descending pleasantly. Below the zigzag, turn sharply left away from the farm, keeping a stone wall on the right, with the river beyond. The grassy track through bracken, across the Wholehope Burn, and contouring round The Knocks, is glorious, especially in autumn. Ahead you will see the route slanting up a hillside, the walk's sting in its tail, although it is not quite so steep as it looks.

The Peth, as it is called, is another historic track. From its superb viewpoint crest continue across a farm track on to rough pasture, eventually picking up a narrow path which descends through bracken to the metalled road above a cattle grid. Follow this down the valley to Alwinton.

## 4. Holystone Oaks (1½ miles-2.4km)

This short walk is included primarily for its natural history interest of old oak woodland, and the intimate landscapes and wildlife of the valley of Dove Crag Burn.

Park in the Forestry Commission car-park and picnic area beyond Holystone village on the road signposted 'Campville'. A large notice-board illustrates a number of walks in the vicinity. Ours is the orange one, and as it is waymarked throughout, no further directions are needed. There are no steep sections, but the path above the south side of Dove Crag Burn, along Lanterside, is narrow and can be slippery after rain. This is a walk to be leisurely and quietly savoured, bearing in mind that Holystone North Wood is a Nature Reserve.

If time and inclination permit, include a visit to Lady's Well, an easy short stroll from Holystone village, or the green waymarked walk from the Forestry Commission car-park.

## 5. Simonside Ridge Walk (3 miles-4.8km)

Relatively short in distance, high in scenic value, with outstanding views in all directions. Choose a clear afternoon with a brisk west or north-west wind: late August for the heather, October for the bracken, and be prepared for some steep bits.

Park in Forestry Commission car-park and picnic area, 042992, along the Garleigh Moor road south of Rothbury, and walk eastwards along the road for ½ mile (805m) – thus getting the road walking over. Turn right, opposite the signpost pointing to 'Cup-and-Ring Stone', and follow a well-defined peaty, stony track up the moorland hillside, aiming for the left-hand end of easternmost outcrop on the ridge ahead. The track swings right, past large boulders of Fell Sandstone.

Views over Coquetdale to distant Cheviots, and eastwards to the coast, are with you all along the moorland path as it heads to the next outcrop, Dove Crag, and then to Simonside itself in another mile. Steep scarp faces on your right add craggy drama to the view, with the plantations of Rothbury Forest below, Rothbury beyond, its backcloth of moor, and the great woodlands of Cragside. Late afternoon sunlight models the far Cheviots, and glows across Coquetdale's fair fields and shelter-belts.

*In the Simonside Hills, looking east along the north-facing escarpment*

Descend carefully the steep, rocky western slopes of Simonside, and turn right on to a good forest track leading steadily down through the forest. Red waymarks are a good guide back to the car-park.

### 6. Rothbury – Coquet Valley – Thropton – Rothbury (6 miles-9.7km)

Fell-side, moorland and valley pastures provide good variety. Steep to start with, then no difficulties.

Car-park on south side of river above bridge. Cross footbridge into town centre and seek narrow passage on north side of Market Street opposite village cross and small green. At first road turn left and right, up another narrow passage. Cross Hillside Road, and climb track ahead up hillside, past new housing, to gate with access to moor. By wood, turn left and keep wall on left as you contour hillside westwards, climbing gradually as you leave the houses of Rothbury below. Good track gradually swings northwards, climbing past Brae Head on to open moor. Turn left through gate in wall, and descend by a good track, probably villagers' access to moorland commons. Pass through three gates, and down road (Physic Lane), past neat stone cottages and a well to main road. Turn right, walk through Thropton village to far end.

Turn left, by Thropton Demesne Farm, and bear left to footbridge over river. Go across pasture south-east with fence to your right, and gradually swing right through a gate, follow hedge upwards to metalled road. Left, and left at road junction, past house 'Summerville' on left, towards the hamlet of Newtown. Turn left at first bend, past houses on right, into a descending lane. This soon turns sharp right, and becomes a good field path with a hedge on the right. Cross Lady's Bridge and continue ahead over a field, through a gate, across a small stream, past gorse bushes up to the road. Turn right, keeping on road for 80yd (73m) to take another path on the right which drops to the river and follows the north bank back to the footbridge by the car-park.

### 7. The Wannie Line Walk (7 miles-11.3km)

This 7-mile route was inaugurated in 1987 by The National Trust, and provides a circular walk through beautiful and historic landscapes by incorporating sections of two disused railway lines and crossing part of the Trust's 13,000 acre (5,261ha) Wallington Estate. It lies just outside the eastern boundary of the National Park, starting and finishing at The National Trust Regional Office at Scot's Gap, 12 miles (19.3km) south of Rothbury, 038866.

*The track down to Thropton from Rothbury Moor*

The route, reasonably level throughout, is clearly waymarked with white arrows, and runs in an anticlockwise direction, first heading north along the track of the old Rothbury line. After 2 miles (3.2km), it reaches the Delf Burn and follows a burnside path westwards. Emerging from woodland, with medieval field strips on Toot Hill to the south, it loops southwards through an old limestone quarry, passes a fine group of limekilns built about 1860 and swings northwards. Notice the tall earth dykes faced with drystone walling, and capped with now-overgrown hedges. These 'sod casts' were field boundaries created by Sir Walter Blackett in the early eighteenth century. The beech trees are probably contemporary with the old dyke.

Turning westwards to cross the B6342 south of Gallow Hill, and continuing as a field path, the route heads for a small plantation where it turns southwards, following field boundaries where more 'sod casts' can be identified, until it joins the 'Wannie Line', the former Wansbeck railway for a 2-mile (3.2km) level walk eastwards to Scot's Gap.

## 8. Roman Wall (4 miles-6.4km)

This four-mile walk includes the most scenically dramatic section of the Roman Wall along the impressive Whin Sill crags above Crag Lough. The National Trust, which owns this stretch, carries out much excavation, restoration and repair work to the Wall and its accompanying footpath, and the track is often diverted. Please follow these diversions.

Start and finish at the Steel Rigg car-park, *751677*, on the line of the Wall, 1/2 mile (805m) north of B6318 at Once Brewed. Late afternoon sunlight illuminates the crags, adding to the enjoyment of majestic and historic scenery. Turn right (NW) from the car-park, down a hill, and right again at the bottom over a ladder stile, waymarked 'Hotbank'. Walk eastwards along good farm track, past the birches and Scots pines of Peatrigg Plantation. Continue past Peatrigg barn, over two ladder stiles, following waymark signs, and keeping to the footpath where it crosses hay-meadows. Bear right at a small sike (stream) and aim for the eastern end of Hotbank Crags, through a gate and along a cart track to Hotbank Farm. A good view of Crag Lough is revealed here. Go through another gate, across the farmyard, over a stile, turning right on to the line of the Wall, followed here by the Pennine Way.

Milecastle 38, overgrown, has an explanatory panel beside it. Continue along the Wall, over two ladder stiles, and climb the track beside the Wall as it rises through a small wood of Scots pines and sycamore to the open top of the crags above Crag Lough, where rowan, hazel and bracken have found footholds. From here back to the car-park is 1 1/2 miles (3.6km) of sheer delight, with history beneath your boots and at your shoulder, and superb views northwards over Crag Lough to lonely uplands and distant, dark plantations, southwards over the softer landscapes of the South Tyne and beyond to the northern Pennines. All sky and space and splendour, and a westerly breeze in your face. The Wall's course is undulating, and though the ups and downs are steep, they are short. Steepest are near the end of the walk where a stony staircase descends the western end of Peel Crags, where (1987) much excavation is in process. Follow the footpath signs back to Steel Rigg car-park in its small wood.

### 9. Allen Banks (3 miles-4.8km)

Paths follow both banks of the River Allen for much of its course in the gorge. Notices in the National Trust car-park in the former walled garden of Ridley Hall, 796643, a mile east of Bardon Mill, shows these clearly, but on the ground they are not waymarked. However, it is easy to devise a circular route of about 3 miles (4.8km) incorporating riverside and woodland tracks. These are likely to be muddy after rain.

Walk south from the car-park on the west bank, choosing the lower path if you favour riverside scenery, or the upper one for more open views over valley and parkland. This upper path passes Briarswood Banks Nature Reserve before joining the lower one near Plankey Mill Farm, where you cross the river by a wooden suspension bridge. Climb the road past the farm and turn left along a field path back to the river, where in summer broom and wild flowers add a riot of colour. As the river enters its gorge opposite Raven Crag the path climbs steeply into deciduous woodland where ferns and mosses thrive, and rhododendrons add summer colour. Eventually a path descends to river level where another suspension bridge leads over to the west bank and the path back to the car-park.

### 10. Blanchland – Shildon – Pennypie – Baybridge – Blanchland (4miles-6.4km)

Historic village, lead-mining survivals, open moorland, a drove road and a stretch of the Derwent valley provide sustained interest and wide views in a short, easy walk of four miles.

Start and finish at the big car-park by the old school in Blanchland, and turn left on to a minor road heading northwards, following a burn first on your right, later on the left. After plantations on the right the lane climbs to the old lead-mining settlement of Shildon. Spoil-heaps behind the cottages, the ruins of the only remaining Cornish engine-house in the north and the smelt-mill chimney, are melancholy memorials of the industry which ceased here a century ago.

Keeping left where the lane forks, the track climbs steadily past Sitka spruce plantations, across more open pastures above Shildon Burn. Soon, Pennypie House appears, backed by wide moorland. The building was probably a drovers' inn, with smithy, where southbound Scottish cattle could be shod. Go through the first gate before the farm, ignoring track to the house, and go through another gate ahead, left to a plank ·bridge over a stream, on to a moorland track southwards. In clear weather the view ahead to the northern Pennines is superb. One wonders whether the drovers appreciated these. The distant chimney is three crow-flying miles away, and Bolt's Law beyond reaches 1770ft (540m).

Go through gate at moor end, down steep hill on gravelly track, to Baybridge in the Derwent valley. Keep right at the road junction, past the picnic site on the right, and immediately before the bridge, take the waymarked riverside footpath on the left along the north bank of the Derwent to Blanchland.

# GAZETTEER

*Asterisk denotes fuller discussions in main text*

**\*Akeld**  Farm-hamlet below Humbleton Hill west of Wooler, with a sixteenth-century bastle-house contributing to atmosphere of isolated settlement with needs of defence. Good walks into the sheltering hills.

**Allen Banks** (National Trust)  Mile-long wooded gorge of the River Allen in the South Tyne valley. Best access to miles of woodland and riverside walks is the National Trust car-park and picnic area in former walled garden of Ridley Hall, on minor road off A69 one mile (1.6km) east of Bardon Mill. Rhododendrons add colour in early summer, but early spring and late autumn are probably more rewarding times to follow riverbank and upland paths.

**Allendale Town**  A sundial on St Cuthbert's church records the latitude of 54' 60", which places it midway between Cape Wrath and Beachy Head, thus meriting Allendale's claim (contested by Hexham) to be the geographical centre of Britain. It was, in the eighteenth and nineteenth centuries, a busy centre of north Pennine lead-mining, and most buildings date from then, loosely grouped round large Market Place heavy with horse-chestnuts, copper beeches, sycamores and a triangle of limes planted to mark Queen Victoria's 1887 Jubilee.

The many inns and hotels testify to the thirsty nature of lead-mining. All those along north side of Market Place are or were inns, with The King's Head a former coaching-inn, in continuous use since the eighteenth century. Nearby, St Cuthbert's church is a mid-Victorian replacement of an earlier building. Island of buildings in the centre of the Market Place includes the Hearse House, while the present Post Office has been a variety of shops for over a century. The adjacent Tea Rooms was a pub in 1870. All are of grey-brown local stone.

Allendale's most impressive buildings are the Savings Bank of 1875, on the east side of the Market Place, and the Hotspur Hotel on the south side, bow-windowed and also with a pedimented doorway, probably a century older. Nearby, The Old Oaks was formerly The Rose and Crown, and with its low-beamed ceilings and stone floors, was a typical hostelry. Rows of miners' cottages, 1845, beyond Dawson Place, represent Allendale's industrial vernacular buildings, as does the arched entrance to the famous Blackett Level, at the foot of the hill on which the church stands, and reached by a riverside path from The Peth, the hill descending north-westwards from the Market Place. Water pumps in the Market Place (Isaac's Well) and in Shield Street were erected by a local travelling grocer, Isaac Holden, around 1850.

Peaty burns tumble down from surrounding moors to supplement the East Allen; packhorse tracks lead over the moors, towards Hexham, the Devil's Water, and Blanchland in the Derwent valley. Smelt-mill flues and stacks are stark symbols of the vanished industry, and in the dark days of winter a festival with pagan origins commemorates a more distant, primitive past. On New Year's Eve a lively bonfire blazes in the Market Place and men called (for that night) Guisers, wildly dressed and painted with blackened faces, and carrying barrels of burning tar, march in festival procession round the town. Thus the Allendale Baal Fire sees out each old year.

*Allenheads  Lead-mining settlement podded at head of East Allen valley in wild north-Pennine country. Embowered, irregular village square with small green, a few stone houses, pub, flower-laden gardens, and former mine buildings, workshops, offices. The hills are riven with old workings, quiet for a century. Former miners' tiny farms are either holiday cottages or derelict, and plantations soften the landscape's austerity.

Alnham  Typical Northumbrian hamlet based on fifteenth-century pele-tower now a private house. Norman church largely rebuilt 1870. Nearby hills have hill forts, old field systems, cairns and hut sites, and plenty of good tracks for walkers who like a sense of history with their solitudes.

*Alwinton (pronounced Allenton)  Small village in Coquetdale, beautifully situated beneath Cheviot foothills, and facing south to heathery Harbottle hills. Meeting-place of ancient routes gave village strategic and historic importance, but tranquility has replaced turbulence. Hosedon Burn bisects a green, with a few stone cottages and houses along one side, together with splendid pub, Rose and Thistle, the Post Office, and a farm. Car-park and toilets are asset for visitors, and St Michael's church, below village, is interesting and unusual, its hillside position necessitating ten steps rise from nave to chancel.

Annual Shepherds' Show (second Saturday in October), very much a local gloriously homely affair, in idyllic setting. Confined to shepherds, sheep, and rural skills rather than Range Rovers and green wellies. Fell-racers, wrestlers, trail-hounds, stick-carvers, home cooking, and garden produce, complement sounds of Northumbrian pipes, local dialect, and sheep voices to delight the senses, as autumn burnishes bracken on surrounding hills.

Aydon Castle (English Heritage)  On rolling, wooded slopes above Tyne valley, north of Corbridge, superb example of medieval, fortified manor house. Modest in scale, little changed through centuries, splendidly evokes domestic living conditions of early fourteenth century, and of use as farmhouse from seventeenth century to 1960.

*Alwinton*

**Bellingham** (pronounced Bellinjum)   Small market town and 'capital' of north Tynedale, serving wide area of remote hill country. As nearest town to Kielder Water, it has increased tourist importance, but character remains same, with grey stone buildings of little architectural pretensions, along a wide main street, and round the Square which is a rectangle, with many pubs; Black Bull oldest, Rose and Crown largest. St Cuthbert's church, tucked away at southern end of main street, claims most attention. During the troubled centuries, it was frequently burned, but thirteenth-century chancel survived. Rebuilding and remodelling of 1609 gave it a remarkable roof of heavy stone slabs supported in nave and transept by twenty-two transverse arches of stone, giving strong, almost primitive medieval character, as well as reducing fire-risk. Churchyard stones commemorate Northumbrian Dodds, Milburns, Charltons. Robsons, as well as foes like Armstrongs and Elliots. Long stone slab in grass said to be grave of pedlar who featured in unusual local robbery over 200 years ago. St Cuthbert's Well, between church and river, is stone pillar or pant, with water emerging from spout, probably late Georgian origin. May replace earlier spring associated with famous saint. Ironstone in nearby hills brought industry to Bellingham middle of last century. Pennine Way, and appeal of hill country around, brings walkers and other visitors today. Former great annual wool fair replaced now by lively, important agricultural show, last Saturday in August.

**Billsmoor**   Along the upper part of the Grasslees valley, by the B6341 between Rothbury and Elsdon, former medieval deerpark retains semi-natural birch-alder woodland on southern slopes, interspersed with rocks, heather and grass, with northern side enclosed and grazed, as are the flat riverside haughs. Eighteenth-century farmhouses built on to pele-towers, and at Billsmoorfoot part of the 7-mile (11.2km) deerpark wall, built early last century, adjoins the road. Good views from top of the road, and at Billsmoor viewpoint car-park.

**Black Middens Bastle-House**   Lonely in the valley of the Tarset Burn 7 miles (11km) north-west of Bellingham, now owned by English Heritage, this is Northumberland's only example of a bastle-house with free public access. Although roofless, the structure has been restored and made safe. Dates probably from late sixteenth century, as a fortified farmhouse.

**Blanchland**   In the upper Derwent valley, and on the Northumberland bank of the river, justifiably regarded as one of the county's most attractive villages, a paradox and a tiny paradise. Trees clothe the lower moorland slopes sheltering the village in its valley setting. Trim rows of buff-coloured stone cottages line sides of a large square bisected by a road. In 1747 John Wesley described Blanchland as 'little more than a heap of ruins'. Five years later the trustees of Lord Crewe's estate (he was one of the great Durham prince-bishops) completely restored the old settlement, retaining its original monastic layout.

Blanchland Abbey was founded 1169 by White Canons, and parts of the thirteenth-century abbey church survive as the parish church, while refectory and guest-house are incorporated into the Lord Crewe Arms. Former gatehouse is handsome focal-point in the village square and now contains a shop. Stone cottages were for lead-miners working nearby mines, thus making Blanchland surely one of the earliest and most attractive of industrial villages.

**Border Mires**   Remotely-situated in Wark Forest, west of Stonehaugh, fragmentary mire system of relict peat bogs and fens, with extensive carpets of sphagnum moss and other rare bog plants. They appear unspectactular and dull, but the close view reveals unsuspected riches of colour. Haining Head Moss is wet and rich in plants; Comb Rigg Moss, being drier, has heather. Most have cranberry, bog asphodel and sundew. Together they form a site of international importance, and are either national or local nature reserves, leased from the Forestry Commission.

**Branxton**   Nearest village to Flodden Field, site of the worst of Anglo-Scottish battles. Amid rolling cornfields below northern foothills of Cheviots, a tall Celtic cross, erected 1910, bears simple inscription 'Flodden 1513. To the brave of both nations.' Thus are commemorated in a lonely, hauntingly beautiful landscape, 10,000 Scotsmen and 5,000 English – almost the whole of the chivalry of the northern kingdom – who died on two September days. The famous Scottish lament, The Flowers of the Forest, captures the sadness and horror; Scott's *Marmion* also recalls 'Flodden's fatal field'. A short, steepish walk on a surfaced path, leads visitors from a good car-park to the silhouetted cross, a place for quiet thoughts.

**Brinkburn Priory** (English Heritage)   Glorious riverside setting in a wooded bend of the Coquet 4½ miles (7km) south-east of Rothbury, a house for Augustinian canons founded by Bertram lords of Mitford about 1135. Priory suffered repeatedly from Scots attackers, and suppressed 1536. Late twelfth-century church excellently restored and re-roofed in 1858 by Newcastle architect

Thomas Austin. Building is a superb example of transition from Romanesque style to Gothic. Organ has been restored, windows replaced, and church licensed for services. Masonry from domestic buildings re-used for nearby house. Turner's painting of Brinkburn Priory, c1830, now in Sheffield City Art Galleries, shows it ruinous, but captures the tranquil beauty.

**Brocolitia**   Large car-park beside Military Road 4 miles (6.4km) west of Chollerford suggests something worth seeing, but the fort at Carrawburgh (pronounced Carrawbruff) is merely bumps in a grassy rectangle. However, footpath leads to a grassy hollow where foundations of a Mithraic Temple have been excavated and revealed. The three altar stones are fakes, without detracting from this evidence of worship of an Eastern sun-god beneath cool, grey northern skies.

**Byrness**   Post-war village for foresters and their families in Redesdale. Forty-seven houses, shops, school, church and village hall cannot disguise their being a planted community. Small hotel and information centre nearby. Tiny church has some unusual stained glass, showing workmen and machinery, commemorating men who died in building Catcleugh Reservoir up the road. Forestry Drive links Byrness with Kielder, 13 miles (20km) across the watershed to the west. Be warned, the road is not tarmac all the way, but does have fine viewpoints, parking spaces, picnic areas, waymarked walks and nature trails. Well worth the toll charged, and easily the most direct and scenic route between Redesdale and Kielder Reservoir.

**Cambo** (National Trust)   Eighteenth-century planned village on the Wallington estate. Sir Walter Blackett started rebuilding it in 1730, but not until 1911 did Sir George Trevelyan finally convert the old schoolhouse (where Capability Brown attended as a boy) into a village hall. Earlier, Sir Charles Trevelyan cleared many old buildings and constructed the neat terrace of South Row with its colourful gardens. All houses are of good local sandstone. Post office occupies the ground floor of medieval pele-tower. Southwards aspect over calm parklands illustrates serenity of Cambo and its caring owners.

**Carter Bar**   Historically the Redeswire, now, at 1,371ft (418m) the highest point on any main road between England and Scotland. Road signs by the A68 proliferate; wide-ranging views northwards embrace much of the Scottish lowlands, but to the south and west dark plantations spread into the distance. The 'bar' was probably a turnpike gate early last century when this ancient route to Scotland was improved. It is still the only main road across the Cheviots.

**Catcleugh Reservoir**   England's most northerly lake, albeit artificial, completed in 1905 to supply more water for Tyneside. A huge steam-navvy supplemented muscle-power of hundreds of navvies, and horse-drawn carts carried away the boulders, earth and tree-roots. At £4 a week for a 12-hour day Catcleugh navvies were then about the best-paid in Britain. A68 hugs the northern shore for 1½ miles (2.4km), and a public footpath crosses the dam before climbing westwards to the remote wilderness of Kielderhead Moor.

**Cawfields**   North of the Military Road 2 miles (3.6km) above Haltwhistle, an old quarry has been landscaped to form a good car-park and picnic site, showing impressive cross-section of Whin Sill above a small, deep lake. Easy access to good section of Roman Wall, past Milecastle 42, one of the best, on broad foundations with many courses of masonry. Good views of the vallum.

**Chesters** (English Heritage)   West of Chollerford on B6318, well-preserved remains of Roman fort, Cilurnum, in wooded parkland setting by North Tyne. 6-acre (2.4ha) fort housed 500 cavalry, and remains include gateways, barracks, commandant's house, headquarters building, and very impressive baths complex. Museum houses good collection of sculptures and Roman inscriptions.

   On opposite bank of river, accessible by footpath from south side of Chollerford bridge, **Chesters Bridge Abutment** is best surviving example in Britain of masonry apron, now high and dry, which supported Roman bridge across river. Early one may have had four stone arches carrying 20ft (6m) wide road. Successor was timber.

**Cheviot, The**   At 2,676ft (815m) the highest mountain in Northumberland, accessible from College and Harthope valleys. Commonest route is from Langleeford, but most exciting from College valley via Henhole or The Bizzle. Be prepared for wet feet and a disappointing summit – a broad, flat plateau of peat bog, which surprised Defoe in 1728, who expected precipices and a pinnacle. Even now there's only a triangulation column on a grassy mound, sometimes inaccessible because of soggy ground. A climb only for the record, not for pleasure, or the view.

**\*Chew Green**   Lines in a lonely landscape near Coquet Head reveal the extent of a group of Roman marching camps. Three centuries of Roman achievement are insignificant in the grass, seen at close range, but viewed in low-angle sunlight they leap into life. Rome's most northerly outpost merits Sir Ian Richmond's description as 'the most remarkable visible group of Roman earthworks in Britain'.

**Chillingham**   Small village, large fourteenth-century castle remodelled 1625–35, now occasionally open to public. Six hundred-acre (243ha) medieval park is home to rare herd of Chillingham White Cattle, descendants of those trapped when park was walled 1220. Open April-October, but only under supervision of Warden, and no guarantee of seeing animals. St Peter's church, mainly Norman, contains superb tomb, c1450, to Sir Ralph Gray and his wife. Sumptuous artistry, best of its date in the north of England.

**Chollerford**   Robert Mylne's handsome, five-arched bridge, replacing an older one destroyed by floods, carries General Wade's Military Road across the North Tyne. Short riverside path downstream leads to massive stone abutments of Roman bridge, with Cilurnum (Chesters) opposite. Eastwards along the B6318 a stark, wooden cross commemorates site of Battle of Heavenfield, 634, where Northumbrian King Oswald defeated heathen British King Cadwallon. St Oswald's church, north of the road, occupies site where Oswald is said to have erected cross to mark his victory.

**\*Chollerton**   Farm-hamlet on the east side of the North Tyne valley. St Giles' Church, externally unimpressive, has interior surprises, the south arcade of its four-bay nave being Roman columns from Cilurnum (Chesters) across the river. One font is a re-used Roman altar, there is Jacobean woodwork, and tiny organ is by Father Smith, famous seventeenth-century instrument maker. Note unusual carved headstone in churchyard to John Saint, a fuller. Building by gate was stables used by horses of parishioners travelling from distance.

To north, early nineteenth-century buildings are superb example of Northumbrian agricultural equivalent to contemporary colliery village. Late Georgian farmhouse, terrace of labourers' cottages, extensive stables, byres and barns, farm steam-engine chimney, and stone-built tower mill lacking sails.

**\*Clennell Street**   Best-known of all the Border 'streets' or crossings, probably originating as a prehistoric trade route linking Northumbrian outposts of the Votadini with tribal territories to the north. Never Romanised, but used by medieval monks, Border reivers, drovers and smugglers. Now a splendid track for walkers heading northwards from Alwinton to the Cheviot ridge at Windy Gyle. Acquired its name from deserted medieval village of Clennell, near Alwinton.

**\*College Valley**   Pleasant, unspoilt, remote valley penetrating southwards from Glendale into the Cheviot Hills, served by a single-track road beyond Hethpool, accessible to motorists by permit only, obtainable from John Sale and Partners, Estate Agents, 18 Glendale Road, Wooler. Formed by a geological fault, smooth-floored, and enclosed by smooth-sided high green hills, it is always open to walkers (but not skiers). Gravel terraces above valley floor glow with gorse in early summer. On The Bell, below Hethpool, the famous Collingwood oaks, planted early last century, were intended for 'navy timber', but did not thrive. Now managed more successfully by National Park Authority. Fine examples of medieval lynchets near Hethpool and good walks from hamlet. Harder stuff from Mounthooly, near valley head, to The Cheviot, Auchope, The Schil. Henhole and The Bizzle are exciting rock features, with interesting alpine vegetation.

**\*Coquetdale**   The Coquet is Northumberland's longest river, spanning 55 miles (88km) from its source at Coquethead on the England-Scotland border high in the Cheviots to its meeting with the sea at Amble, below Warkworth. Its wild upper valley above Alwinton follows a sinuous course between steep-sided uplands of sheep-cropped grass, heather and bracken. Escaping from its confines it matures and broadens past Harbottle, Holystone and Hepple in a widening vale beneath the northern flanks of the Simonside Hills, to Rothbury, Coquetdale's capital and gateway. Between there and Cragside's woods the river races through the gorge of the Thrum, emerging placidly to Pauperhaugh's graceful bridge, and meandering past Brinkburn Priory to continue a winding course eastwards across flood plain and farmlands.

**Corbridge**   Compact, friendly little town on north bank of Tyne east of Hexham. Agricola recognised strategic importance of site for river crossing where main north-south road crossed important east-west Stanegate. After Legions left their road system dictated military movements in an almost roadless land. Today's trunk road between Newcastle and Carlisle, A69, and the main road north, A68, now bypass Corbridge, to the town's benefit.

Northumbria's Anglian rulers made it a royal burgh with Market Place and nearby parish church its nucleus. Narrow proportions of original building still traceable in masonry of west end of St Andrew's church. Anglo-Saxons used Roman stones from Corstopitum for massive arch between nave and tower. Lower part of tower is probably late eighth century, upper part eleventh, but most of remainder is thirteenth century, by when Corbridge was Northumberland's wealthiest town after Newcastle, which probably says more for the county's poverty than the town's prosperity. King John visited it three times and gave it a charter. The Scots came equally frequently, but merely pillaged and burned it.

Vicar's pele in churchyard, c1300, attests to Border troubles, and to the ready availability of Roman masonry from Corstopitum. Its restored roof has kept it in good order, and interior of building illustrates, given some imagination, what life in a medieval tower-house would have been like. Now, sensibly, houses Tourist Information Office on the ground floor, with museum and display above. A later pele-tower, c1600, adjoins Jacobean Low Hall at eastern end of Main Street.

Small enough to explore easily on foot, Corbridge rewards visitors prepared to saunter and savour its streets and grey stone buildings. Obvious starting-point is Market Place, with two market crosses, a thirteenth-century stone one and the cast-iron pillar, bearing the Percy crescent, presented by the Duke of Northumberland in 1814. The Percy lion adorns the descriptive plaque. Stone trough and fountain is one of many 'pants' in the town, which provided people with water from early years of last century. Simple grid pattern of streets, predominantly east-west, simplify town trail. Shops around Market Place would once have been pleasant terrace houses, as upper storeys testify. Front Street and Middle Street, running east from Market Place, continue the terrace theme, with date panels indicating eighteenth-century building or occupancy on marriage. At the end of Front Street, opposite Narrowgate House, steep, cobbled lane was old approach to medieval bridge, with smithy at bottom. Present bridge, 1674, was only one on Tyne which withstood 1771 floods. Good view of it from riverside path to west, joining line of Carel-Gate which was main highway Corbridge to Carlisle until 1762 when present turnpike was constructed. Carel-Gate enters Market Place via Well Bank, at north-west corner.

Hill Street, at top of Well Bank, runs north of parish church. Width suggests earlier market use for fish and meat, and its eastern end was formerly Shamblegate. Many good eighteenth-century houses there and in Princes Street which runs northwards at its eastern end. By that date, Corbridge's market had faded, although the great annual fair on Stagshaw Bank north of the town, by the Portgate, was last held in 1932. In its heyday a century earlier 100,000 sheep and cattle would be offered for sale, but the coming of the railway in early Victorian times, a mile distant on the south side of the river, and its routing through Hexham, signalled a gradual decline of the fair from its upland setting to a more convenient place in the valley at Hexham.

**Corsenside**   Approached by farm lane from A68, St Cuthbert's church stands solitary in Redesdale's spaciousness. Basically Norman, with later bellcote and homely Georgian windows, its simple appeal is enhanced by splendid churchyard memorials, elegantly embellished, beautifully lettered. A quiet place with wide views, denied by sheltering trees to the nearby seventeenth-century farmhouse.

**Corstopitum**   (English Heritage)   Half a mile (1km) west of Corbridge, established by Agricola as communications centre, military headquarters, supply base, and finally as important Roman depot. Camp survived from AD80 to early fifth century. Site lacks grandeur of Housesteads, but ruins are impressively extensive, including vast storehouse, granaries, military compounds, temples, and civilian structures whose occupants supplied garrison's various needs. Stanegate bisected camp in its east-west course, so Corstopitum was a Roman depot astride a main road. Museum displays finds of many excavations.

**\*Crag Lough**  Most impressive of the Northumbrian loughs, dramatically situated beneath frowning cliffs of Whin Sill, and giving Roman Wall walkers, between Housesteads and Peel Crag, the most memorable views. Ecologically interesting because of succession of plant communities from open water to willow carr and raised bog. Bird life abounds, and climbers enjoy the best rock-climbing in Northumberland.

**Cragside** (National Trust)  Victorian industrialist Sir William Armstrong's wealth and vision transformed 900 acres (360ha) of rough heather moorland, north of Rothbury, into a superb country estate centred on Norman Shaw's remarkable mansion, 1863–83. Millions of trees were planted, miles of drives created, ablaze with rhododendrons and azaleas each June. The house and its contents are a shrine to high Victoriana.

**Doddington**  Compact stone village 3 miles (4.8km) north of Wooler, vastly shrunken in size and importance from medieval times. In early eighteenth

*Cragside, near Rothbury*

century, had weekly cattle market, hand-loom weavers, and an important quarry. Enclosure of Doddington Moor early last century caused village fortunes to ebb. By 1834 only eight farms remained. Today, a few cottages cluster round two large farms, and only the church, the tall pele-tower (called Doddington bastle) and a well survive from more distant days. Good walks on Doddington Moor, Iron Age settlement on Dod Law, and more cup-and-ring markings.

**Edlingham**   East of A697, in valley below Corby's Crags, small village with interesting sequence of buildings surrounded by ridge-and-furrow of medieval ploughlands. Ruins of late fourteenth-century castle, an elaborate tower-house (English Heritage), squat Norman church with rare, tunnel-vaulted porch, late Georgian farmhouses and cottages, and railway viaduct of 1887.

**\*Elsdon**   Historic capital of Redesdale, situated in broad hollow among moorlands, with opening only westwards. Church and graveyard divide large green, elongated north-south, into two parts, the upper smaller and secluded, the lower large and more open. Large, grassy Mote Hills above the ravine of the Elsdon Burn north of the village, formerly Norman motte-and-bailey castle, headquarters of lordship of Redesdale during twelfth century. St Cuthbert's church, fourteenth-century, has unusual vaulting in aisles. Interesting monuments inside, impressive headstones outside, with good, discreet modern ones in local stone, well-lettered.

   Elsdon Tower, c1400, best example of a Vicar's Pele, dominates and is still occupied. Garden open. Victorian Rector's School very modest, as are stone houses, eighteenth and nineteenth century, bordering central and lower green. Stone figure of Bacchus indicates former inn; modern signs, each showing different birds, adorn Bird in the Bush west of green. Circular pinfold adds traditional touch. Elsdon was on old drove road from Scotland to Newcastle, via Chew Green. Today's visitors appreciate tranquil atmosphere, and enjoy best view of village from the Cambo road to the south.

**Featherstone Castle**   Beautifully situated on parkland haughs by South Tyne, graciously wooded. Medieval tower house with Jacobean additions, romanticised in early nineteenth century to give strong Gothic overtones. Riverside path passes park gates where plaque commemorates use of Featherstone Park as POW camp for German officers, 1945–8, whose interpreter, Captain Herbert Sulzbach OBE, dedicated himself to Anglo-German reconciliation.

**Gamel's Path**   Name given to the northern part of Dere Street between Featherwood and Chew Green, now surfaced for military use. Probably a medieval track across the Border, its course supposedly marked by crosses, of which two socket-stones survive, misleadingly called Middle and Outer Golden Pot. Where track descends to Coquet valley, deep hollow ways by roadside are probably result of continuous droving of highland cattle southwards to English fairs and markets.

**\*Gatehouse**   Hamlet in valley of Tarset Burn, north-west of Bellingham, with bastle-houses facing each other across the narrow road. Northerly one, still roofed, is much better-preserved, easily seen from the road.

**Glanton**   Good example of rebuilt rural village following 1763 completion of

Northumberland section of London to Edinburgh coach road through Newcastle and Kelso. For over fifty years it prospered as a commercial centre, yet never acquired an Anglican church. The Red Lion retained its name; the Turk's Head became the Queen's Head at the Jubilee, and West Turnpike recalls the late eighteenth-century road in its wide course through the village.

**Glendale**   Valley and plain below north-east flanks of Cheviot Hills. Below its meeting with the College Burn near Kirknewton, the Bowmont Water becomes the River Glen, flowing past Coupland and Akeld, and meandering northwards to join River Till. Claims site of Saxon palace of Ad Gefrin. Former basin of Glendale lake, now Milfield Plain, is most fertile farmland in Northumberland, where George Culley and others showed what could be achieved, in late eighteenth, early nineteenth centuries. Wooler now the capital of Glendale.

**\*Grasslees Valley**   Most attractive deciduously wooded valley in National Park, where complexes of oak-birch-alder woods enhance stretches of the B6341 between Rothbury and Elsdon. Roadside car-park below Harehaugh encourages more leisurely appraisal, especially of burn-side alders.

**Greaves Ash**   On northern hillside above Linhope in the Breamish valley, extensive remains of prehistoric settlement in and around Iron Age hill fort. Sites of two groups of round, stone-built huts, 27 and 13, probably of Romano-British village.

**Greenhead**   The 'Military Road', B6318, following the National Park's southern boundary across Haltwhistle Common, swoops steeply down to the valley of the Tipalt Burn at Greenhead, a rural, non-commuter village developed from an older settlement, Glenwhelt, when the turnpike was completed in 1753. House with portico at foot of hill was former coaching inn, The Globe. Dobson built Greenhead church in 1826 for £800. Restoration in 1880 cost £1,000.

**Grindon Lough**   Close to south-east corner of National Park, south of B6318, and easily visible from Stanegate. Twenty-two-acre (8.9ha) lake, now Nature Reserve noted for its wildfowl, especially in winter, attracting flocks of greylag, bean and barnacle geese. Regular visitors include whooper and Bewick's swans. Wintering waders as passage-migrants include greenshank, ruff, and black-tailed godwit. No close access; good view from road.

**Haltwhistle**   Small town on north bank of South Tyne. Name has nothing to do with trains, but probably means 'junction of streams by a hill'. Unpretentious but not unattractive in a workaday way. Main Street has gentle curves, better in its eastern half, where a widening forms small rectangular Market Place. Two- and three-storey houses, most ground floors now shops. No outstanding secular buildings, but none too depressing. Red Lion, whitewashed, incorporates tower-house features, corbelling, and at back, part of medieval chimney. Further east, above Haltwhistle Burn, remains of former bastle-house. A few cottages show eighteenth-century date-panels. Many alleys, cobbled and flagged, add to the stony character of the town.

  Holy Cross church, south of Market Place, displays a typically northern, thirteenth-century exterior with lots of lancets, while inside the painted chancel roof may be by Kempe, and some stained glass came from the William Morris factory. Good view south, beyond the bypass, and across the Tyne valley. Light industries help to keep the town alive, following decline of older ones like mining and quarrying.

**\*Harbottle**   Main village in upper Coquetdale. Attractive stone houses line road below the green knowe surmounted by meagre remains of Harbottle Castle. Good pub, craft centre, and, west of village 390 acre (160ha) nature reserve, Harbottle Crags, mainly heather-moorland, with impressive outcrops of Fell Sandstone and associated flora. Waymarked Nature Trail to Drake Stone, fine views down Coquetdale. Good car-parking by Information Centre in Forestry Commission woodland.

**Hareshaw Dene and Linn**   Beauty spot near Bellingham. Hareshaw Burn flows through wooded valley, where local people laid out a footpath early this century leading to waterfall (linn) in rocky amphitheatre at head of gorge. Dark and gloomy beneath high summer's dense canopy of trees, more attractive in spring and late autumn. Path crosses succession of small bridges; some steep sections, and can be muddy. Rich botanical and wildlife interest merit ownership of gorge by National Park Authority.

**\*Harthope Valley**   Beautiful, lonely valley running deep into heart of Cheviot Hills, south-westwards near Wooler. Formed by a geological fault, and smoothed by glacier action. Single-track road, with a steep descent at Skirl Naked, leads only to isolated farms at Langlee and Langleeford. Roadside parking on grassy spaces at Carey Burn and Hawsen Burn. Sheep graze the valley floor which is unenclosed and unimproved because of flooding of Harthope Burn, whose braided course has left terraces where gorse glows in early summer. Willow scrub indicates wet undrained land; conifer plantations are shelter belts. Note numerous circular stells. 12 miles (19.3km) of permissive footpaths link valley to Cheviot, Hedgehope and nearby hills. With existing rights-of-way they provide circular walks of various lengths, signposted and waymarked. Some steep bits, though!

**Haydon Bridge**   Small, unpretentious town now largely bypassed by the re-routed A69, in the South Tyne valley. Medieval bridge replaced by present stone one, 1773, but much altered since then. Haydon Old Church is on hill to north, St Cuthbert's, near river, built 1796 with masonry from old structure. Nearby, to south, Langley Castle, 1369, heavily but sympathetically restored last century, is now country house hotel.

**Hedgehope**   Rounded, most shapely and distinctive of all Cheviot summits, but at 2,348ft (715m) considerably lower than Cheviot itself. Accessible from Harthope and Breamish valleys, but looks better in the view than beneath the feet. Forms part of the granite heart of the Cheviot Hills.

**\*Henhole**   Most impressive ravine in Cheviot range, on western flanks of The Cheviot. Ice-sculpted, steep-sided gorge, watered by youthful College Burn, cascading over small waterfalls below crags and screes where alpine vegetation survives. A wild and lonely place far below Auchope Cairn on Pennine Way and most easily accessible from Mounthooly in College valley.

**Hethpool**  Half-hidden, ivy-covered fifteenth-century pele-tower formed nucleus of later estate at foot of College valley, owned by Collingwood family early last century, and the Admiral planted many oaks. Present Hethpool House and its attractive row of cottages built 1919 on site of 1687 house. Beautiful valley and hill scenery in this northernmost neck of National Park.

**Hexham**  The southern and eastern gateway to the National Park, Hexham is one of the most satisfying 'abbey towns' of northern England, developing as a settlement at the gates of Wilfrid's church and its successors, on the south bank of the Tyne. Before it expanded southwards up the steep hillside it must have appeared a very compact group in its riverside setting, a view still to be seen from the Allendale road, B6305, or better still, the Racecourse road at the top of the hill.

The new dual-carriageway A69, keeping north of the river well away from the town, sends out a spur across Mylne's nine-arched bridge of 1785–8, which gives the most rewarding view of Hexham, best seen on a late evening in summer. Before a modern cinema ruined it, the prospect was both Italianate and medieval, the skyline dominated by Hexham Abbey, the Prison, and the Moot Hall.

Wilfrid's building dated from 675–80, and in the following year Hexham became the see of a bishop, remaining so until 821 when the area between Tees and Aln was reunited with Lindisfarne. Today's church, at the heart of a thriving market and commuter town with a 10,000 population, is that of the Augustinian priory founded in 1113, although the building itself is of two periods, 1180–1250 for the nave aisles and transepts, and 1850–1910 for Dobson's east end and Temple Moore's nave. From Wilfrid's time, and now in the chancel of the priory church, roughly above its original place in the apse of the Saxon church, is Wilfrid's throne, the Frith Stool, a tub-shaped stone chair with solid arms, doubtless as uncomfortable as it looks. Steps lead down from the centre of the nave into the finest Anglo-Saxon crypt in England, constructed of Roman masonry from Corstopitum. Niches held oil-lamps, illuminating with feeble flickering flames the faltering steps of the faithful to the sacred relics once displayed here.

Architecturally, the Early English transepts are Hexham's great glory, seen either from outside or within the grey walls. The south transept contains the unique Night Stair leading down from the now-vanished canons' dormitory to the central crossing and pulpitum screen. Today, choristers move down it in procession from their robing chamber into the chancel for each service.

Hexham Priory has been for centuries, and continues to be, the focus of the community, and the centre of religious life for a wide area known as Hexhamshire. Its bell called people to service, and it also called them to arms, particularly during the troubled centuries to 1600. Immediately to the east of the church Hexham's Market Place represents the town's medieval trading nucleus. A weekly market (now Tuesdays and Saturdays) and two fairs were established by 1239, with increasing concentration on the sale of grain and livestock, the cattle market becoming famous during the eighteenth century, and continuing to prosper.

The town's historic core, including the narrow streets radiating from the Market Place as they did in medieval times, together with the Abbey precincts and grounds, and the splendid open area to the south-west called the Sele, are a Conservation Area. As with all small country towns it needs to be explored on foot, leisurely, and preferably with one of the excellent Walkabout Guides or leaflets obtainable at the Tourist Information Office now housed in the Manor Office.

This imposing building, constructed in 1330 as England's first purpose-built prison, formed the Manor Office of the Regality of Hexhamshire, a semi-independent territory administered by the bailiffs of the Archbishop of York. Now, in addition to the Tourist Office, it also houses the Middle March Museum illustrating the history of the Border Country down the centuries. Between it and the Market Place the Moot Hall, a tower-house dating probably from the late fourteenth or early fifteenth century, and formerly the residence of the Archbishop of York's representatives. Courts were held there until 1838. Beyond these medieval buildings is the Old Grammar School, dated 1684, although it was founded in 1599. The building is now a private house.

In the Market Place are the covered Shambles provided by the lord of the manor, Sir Walter Calverley Blackett, in 1769. Stone pillars support the roof on its outer side, wooden ones on the inner side. Nearby, Fore Street, pedestrianised since 1972, is Hexham's main shopping street, and retains a few old shop fronts, notably that of Law's grocery store, formerly 'The Old Pharmacy'. Its elaborate carving, painted black and red, dates from 1918 but looks much older. At its southern end Fore Street meets Battle Hill, formerly the main road through the town, and until the late 1930s the site of twice-yearly stock-fairs, and scene of hirings of servants and agricultural labourers. The Cattle Market is now on the southern side of Battle Hill. Priestpopple to its east has good Victorian buildings, while the Midland Bank of 1896 at the end of Fore Street shows the neatest way of utilising a small triangular area. Its rounded northern end has a frieze in red sandstone illustrating, among other things, our former coinage – pennies, shillings and sovereigns.

St Mary's Chare, a narrow street leading back to the Market Place, should be pedestrianised. It contains a former coaching inn, The George and Dragon, now a fishing-tackle shop. The Grapes Inn bears the Dacre family arms, and a small back door of Woolworth's is certainly seventeenth century. An arch of thirteenth-century St Mary's parish church, embedded in a back wall of a Market Place property, is another survivor of medieval Hexham.

Market Street, funnelling north-westwards from Market Place, was the old way into Hexham, and has good Georgian buildings, now shops, and a few older ones whose doorheads indicate their seventeenth-century date. Opposite St Wilfrid's Gate, 1140, the main entrance to the Priory, is one of the town's best classical buildings, now Government offices. To its west, Market Street becomes Gilesgate, with, at the bottom, a conduit and a Tudor-style house dated 1657.

The main street from the Market Place, running south from the east end of the Abbey, is a later addition to Hexham's townscape. Beaumont Street was built about 1860 to link the main road with the Market Place, destroying some medieval buildings in the process. Nevertheless, its treelined facade opposite the park is dignified, with the Queen's Hall – built as Town Hall and Corn Exchange – quite outstanding. Motorists appreciate roadside parking so close to the Abbey and Market Place. Here, and throughout the town, details delight in doors and windows, in textural contrasting stonework of different dates spanning six centuries, with most buildings of small-town scale, deep-rooted in an historic past, sanctified in the surviving simplicity of Wilfrid's Saxon church.

**High Rochester** (pronounced 'Roe-chester') Much-reduced village built within the ruins of Roman fort of Bremenium, whose origins can still be identified in squared masonry of fallen towers and fragmented walls. Former pele-towers incorporated into houses. From beyond the village, higher viewpoint reveals the Roman site more conspicuously. Former village school of Rochester has porch wholly of Roman stones, with ballistae projectiles for decoration.

**\*Holystone** Charming small village in Coquetdale named after priory of twelfth-century Augustinian nuns. Lady's Well, short walk from village, used in early Christian baptisms here, still provides local water supply from large quiet pool in wooded grove with statue and cross. Waymarked walks from Forestry Commission car-park by Campville road to Lady's Well or Holystone North Wood, a Nature Reserve, mainly of sessile oaks, bracken and mosses. Holystone Burn, more distant, has wider range of vegetation, with juniper, oak and birch. Good village pub, The Salmon.

**Horsley** By A68 north-west of Otterburn. Holy Trinity erected as chapel-of-ease in 1844 and has Roman altar in porch. Memorials in church to first and second barons Redesdale, whose more recent descendants included the famous Mitford sisters.

**\*Housesteads Fort** (National Trust and English Heritage) Most dramatically-situated and most-visited of Hadrian's Wall forts, and probably with most extensive remains. Covers 5 acres (2ha), with north wall incorporated into Hadrian's Wall. Classic layout, with rounded corners, impressive gateways, foundations of granaries, barrack-blocks, headquarters, internal streets, and a twenty-four-seater flushing latrine. Excellent museum displays, explains, interprets Roman discoveries and Wall life.

Fort is half-mile (800m) walk and climb from car-park and Visitor Centre by Military Road, B6318, but really worth it. Housesteads *is* unique. In good weather the views are superb, too.

**Humshaugh** In a loop of the North Tyne near Chollerford, modern housing developments create a misleading impression, for much of the village was built to re-house some of the inhabitants of nearby Haughton whose homes were demolished in 1816 to make way for the castle park.

**Ilderton** A few miles south of Wooler, an excellent example of a self-contained medieval farm-town rebuilt in the eighteenth and nineteenth centuries, with single farm and its associated massive buildings. Contemporary church in pink sandstone.

**Ingram** 'Frontier' village now shrunken from medieval times in Breamish valley on eastern edge of Cheviots. St Michael's church, tree-hidden above the stony river, has Norman foundations and tower with defensive characteristics. National Park Information Centre nearby, good access land by river for parking and picnicking, with enticing paths to surrounding hills and up valley, attracts summer and weekend crowds.

**Kielder**   Late eighteenth-century castle built by Duke of Northumberland as a shooting lodge; now headquarters of Forestry Commission's operations, and interpretative and information centre for public. 1950's forestry village at heart of Kielder Forest comprising Kielder, Wark, Falstone and Redesdale forests yielding 100,000 tonnes of wood a year for industry. Scores of miles of walks and trails through an increasing variety of wildlife habitats. Forest rangers lead guided walks during summer. Motorists may like the challenge of Kielder Forest Drive (toll) linking Kielder with Byrness in Redesdale, a relatively easy way of experiencing forest atmosphere and remoteness.

Kielder Water, opened 1982, covering 2,684 acres (1070ha) is northern Europe's largest man-made lake in Europe's largest man-made forest, and has a 27-mile (43km) shoreline. Controversy about need for a reservoir, to meet north-east's water requirements into next century, now replaced by recognition of its recreational value. Visually lightens landscape gloom of blanketing plantations. New road above southern margin gives occasional good views over lake. Tower Knowe provides wide range of information, car-parks and many facilities, and jetty for ferry trips to north shore. Leaplish, 3½ miles (5.6km) west along road, is main activity centre catering for all major water sports, plus lakeside and woodland walks, forest playground for children, caravan and camp site. Angling facilities from bank or boat at Matthews Linn nearby, and at many beats around shore.

Kielder's southern shore is for the general visitor. North shore, being more remote, is for the more adventurous and experienced, access being via dam road to Hawkhope car-park. Bakethin Reservoir, at Kielder's northern 'tail', is a Nature Reserve, with priority for conservation. Access by foot from 'last' car-park before Kielder village, also leads to splendid skew viaduct on old North Tyne Railway, superb viewpoint.

**Kilham**   Tiny village – really a farm-town – on northern edge of the National Park, above the Bowmont Water. Single long row of single-storey cottages, yellow-painted, against green backcloth of Cheviot foothills.

**Kirk Yetholm**   Over Scottish border, pleasantly situated in valley of Bowmont Water. Merits inclusion not only because it is the northern end of the Pennine Way, but is a quiet, attractive village with neat cottages around a tree-lined green. Long-distance walkers may find the hospitality of the Border Hotel of greater interest.

**Kirkharle**   The 'Corn Road' of 1750 (now B6342) crosses Northumberland's heartlands, passing south of Kirkharle where Sir William Loraine had earlier improved his estates. Lancelot Brown, born on the Kirkharle estate in 1716, was apprentice gardener when sixteen, and there learnt those skills which he put to such good use later in his career. Commemorated locally only in the civilised, mature landscapes with their trees and woodlands, and, more recently, by a simple roadside memorial stone.

*Kielder Water, near Leaplish*

**\*Kirknewton**   One of a succession of small villages situated along the northern foot of the Cheviots, just above the flood levels of Milfield Plain, sited to have a balanced husbandry of fertile land and hill-grazings. Church has remarkable vaulted chancel and transept, and contains unusual medieval sculpture depicting Adoration of the Magi. But it is the rhythm of the hills that dominates.

**Langleeford**   Farm on river terrace at head of Harthope valley with good tracks radiating to surrounding hills, including The Cheviot. Mentioned 1552 in connection with night watches for marauding Scots. Sir Walter Scott said to have spent holiday there 1791, fishing, walking and appreciating pretty dairymaid who brought him goat's-whey each morning. Much inbye land around farm planted with conifer belt for shelter.

**Linhope Spout**   Attractive waterfall where Linhope Burn cascades from an outcrop of Cheviot granite into a rocky basin graced by birches and bracken, all gold and silver in late autumn. Nearest car-park at Hartside, in Breamish valley. Paths continue beyond waterfall to Dunmoor and Hedgehope.

**Lordenshaw**   Easily accessible archaeological remains on heather moorland near Rothbury. Bronze Age burial mounds, cup-and-ring stones, and ramparts of Iron Age hill-fort emphasise continued importance of this area for prehistoric peoples. Modern visitors appreciate the freedom, sense of mystery, and wide views of Coquetdale.

**\*Old Bewick Hill**   Iron Age stronghold above the Vale of Till, with extensive views westwards to Cheviots. Below, among trees, delightful small Norman church of nave and chancel, with rich carving. Founded by Queen Matilda, wife of Henry I, in memory of her father, Malcolm of Scotland, killed at Alnwick. Later owned by Tynemouth Priory. Bridleway leads from hamlet to deserted farm, melancholy-named Blawearie.

**Once Brewed**   National Park Information Centre, with good car-park, near Military Road. Excellent interpretative exhibition. Nearby, north of road, Steel Rigg car-park (NT) is popular starting (or finishing) point for Wall walking, eastwards to Crag Lough and Housesteads, westwards to Winshields. By the main road are Once Brewed Youth Hostel and Twice Brewed Inn.

**Otterburn**   Formerly remote Redesdale hamlet increased in importance early last century with improved roads. Now the A696 carries much Newcastle–Scotland traffic, and the Percy Arms and Otterburn Towers are popular hotels. Otterburn Mill, owned by the Waddell family since 1817, no longer makes the famous Otterburn tweeds, but is open to the public as a showroom where they are still sold. In woodland strip a mile west of village, Percy's Cross marks the spot where Henry Percy (Hotspur) is said to have slain his foe, Earl of Douglas, during the Battle of Otterburn 13 August 1388. Contradictions abound about the battle, and site of encounter between English and Scottish armies has not been proved. As 'Chevy Chase' it has passed into Border folklore and tradition. Some of the dead were taken to Elsdon churchyard for burial. Uplands north of Otterburn acquired for military training in 1911–12 substantially added to, 1940–4 and 1951–4, and closed to the public for about 300 days each year.

**\*Redesdale**   Small brown burns tumble down from remote Border hills to swell the River Rede in its scenic course from Carter Bar to the North Tyne at Redesmouth. Ancient woodlands are dwarfed by huge areas of conifer plantations, but vast areas of tawny uplands remain. Rich humus of history animates contrasting landscapes with prehistoric settlers, Roman soldiers, raiders, reivers, drovers, farmers, miners, and travellers of today. Battles were fought where now the modern army trains, and the Pennine Way threads its moorland way northwards from Bellingham to Chew Green.

**Redesmouth** (REEDSMOUTH on old railway timetables)   Hamlet above the confluence of River Rede with the North Tyne 2 miles (3.2km) south-east of Bellingham. As western terminus of Wansbeck Railway (1862) from Morpeth, it formed a junction with the Border Counties Line. Survived until the 1950s for passengers, 1963 for freight.

**Rory's Still**   A few grey boulders mark the site of an illicit kiln for drying malted barley, on the Inner Hare Cleugh near Davidson's Linn, above Uswayford, in a remote valley north of Coquet. Association and legend are better than reality, and nearby plantations are gloomily enveloping.

**Ross Castle**   Not really a castle but an Iron Age hill-fort in the heather above the woods of Chillingham. The National Trust now owns this 1,033ft (315m) Fell Sandstone escarpment, probably the best viewpoint for eastern and north-eastern sector of the Cheviots, well worth the short climb from the road nearby.

**\*Rothbury**   Capital of Coquetdale lying along and above the north bank of the river, with spacious views across valley to Simonside Hills. Once a popular health resort and small market town, has now become increasingly important as touring and holiday centre. Stone houses line both sides of main street, graced with sloping greens and trees. Buildings along north side form remarkable continuous but varied unbroken frontage. Parish church rather hidden but has its own treasure, a font embodying finely-carved Saxon cross-shaft. Excellent National Park Information Centre nearby, although Rothbury is just outside the Park. Riverside, woodland and moorland walks abound. Good local shops and accommodation to suit all tastes add to Rothbury's appeal.

**St Cuthbert's Cave** (National Trust)   Amid woodland on the Kyloe Hills between Doddington and Belford, accessible by bridlepath from Holburn, impressive cave in sandstone crags where the body of the saint is said to have rested during its long wanderings from Lindisfarne to Durham. Extensive views westwards over rich farmlands to the Cheviots.

**Simonburn**   Before the Conquest, Simonburn parish stretched from the Roman Wall to the Scottish Border, and not until 1811 was it sub-divided into five new parishes of Wark, Bellingham, Thorneyburn, Greystead and Falstone, together with Simonburn itself. In 1832 chapelry of Humshaugh and Haughton was further added. Mid-Victorian restoration of St Mungo's church has not wholly destroyed thirteenth-century ethos. Fragmentary remains in the porch include Anglian survivals – a cross-shaft and boss, and hog-back tombs – and good monuments

*Rothbury, from the north*

inside include one to Cuthbert Ridley, 1625, while the Allgood family vault was beneath the chancel.

Village largely a 1760 estate creation replacing older one destroyed in making of Lancelot Allgood's Nunwick Hall and park. Single-storey, pale colour-washed cottages face a large, chestnut-dominated green against a backdrop of splendid trees. Hawksmoor may have designed the front of the 1725 Rectory, and the tiny tithe-barn nearby has been sympathetically converted into a private house. Northumbrian villages are rarely charming; Simonburn is an exception.

**\*Simonside Hills**   Heather-covered ridge of Fell Sandstone, forming high crags with inward-facing scarp slopes looking across fertile lowlands of Coquetdale near Rothbury, towards Cheviots. Named from distinctive summit in the range, 1,409ft (430m), where outcrops offer scope for rock-climbing, and reward mere mortal walkers with wide-ranging views over the Forestry Commission plantations below the crest.

**Steng Gibbet (Winter's Gibbet)**   South-east of Elsdon, and near National Park's Battlefield Viewpoint, wooden effigy of a head hangs from roadside gibbet, gruesomely commemorating William Winter, gipsy, tried and executed at Newcastle 1791 for murder of an old woman. His corpse was hanged in chains here, in sight of his victim's house.

**Stonehaugh**   The only Forestry Commission village within the National Park area – thirty-five houses built in the early 1950s. Situation, in the upper valley of the Wark Burn, on the eastern edge of Wark Forest, more attractive than appearance. Forest walks abound, and a small, limited-facilities camp site is useful base for visitors prepared to withstand summer midges.

**Tarset** The Tarset Burn, born amid wild moorland scenery above Kielder Forest, flows through plantations before taking a more open course to join the North Tyne between Bellingham and Falstone. A natural route for raiders, it has several ruined bastle-houses, including Black Middens and Gatehouse. Little remains of Tarset Castle near the junction with the Tyne, built 1267 by John Comyn.

**Thirlwall** Stark ruin high above the Tipalt Burn, Thirlwall Castle is an early fourteenth-century pele-tower built with Roman masonry, which explains the absence of any impressive Wall remains nearby. Inhabited by the de Thirlwalls until the eighteenth century, when last heiress married into the Swinburn family, and castle sold to the Earl of Carlisle. South wall fell into burn in 1831, near where Pennine Way crosses it on footbridge near a group of attractive cottages.

**Thropton** Neat stone houses line both sides of street, and near west end Thropton Tower, a fifteenth-century pele, has been converted to a modern residence. Near the Cross Keys another inn, The Three Wheat Heads, hints at the corn-growing capability of mid-Coquetdale. At east end of the village, Physic Lane climbs past flowered cottages and a drinking-well, becoming a green track leading to unenclosed moorland of rocks and heather.

**\*Vindolanda** Short distance south of the National Park Information Centre at Once Brewed, this Roman fort was part of earlier defence system guarding route of the Stanegate through the Tyne corridor. Civilian settlement has yielded significant finds, and continues to do so as excavation continues. The Vindolanda Trust has constructed a replica of a section of the Roman Wall, together with a milecastle and turret.

**Wall** North of Hexham, just off the A6079, Wall's houses, mainly late seventeenth century, are grouped impressively round the sides of a large square green, with a nineteenth-century church and reading-room in the middle. The strict formality suggests early organisation, perhaps defensive in character, either mutual co-operation or by a Norman overlord.

**Wallington** The 'Wallington Beasts' grin at passing travellers. Seventeenth/ eighteenth-century house with 13,000 acres (5,200ha) countryside given to National Trust by Sir Charles Trevelyan, 1941. House built 1688 by Sir William Blackett, remodelled by Daniel Garrett for Sit Walter Blackett 1728–77. Passed to Sir Walter Trevelyan, 1853, whose wife Pauline employed John Dobson to roof in hitherto open courtyard (on Ruskin's advice) which now houses impressive pre-Raphaelite decor, including William Bell Scott's 'Scenes from Northumbrian History'.

Fine furnishings, plasterwork, porcelain, Museum of Curiosities and Dolls' Houses Collection, together with walled garden, mature woodlands, river walk, add to Wallington's grace and elegance.

**Warden** On a neck of land above the meeting of the two Tynes, the Celtic hill-fort of 'Weard-dun', or watch-hill, commanded two valleys long before the Legion built the nearby Wall. An oval churchyard reinforces the idea of parochial antiquity; a seventh-century cross near the church tower may have been a boundary sanctuary cross associated with Hexham Priory, while the tower itself is mainly late Saxon, with a later top storey and a nave-arch of Roman stones. The plain barrel-nave dates from 1765, contemporary with early paper-mills, buildings of which survive in the village.

**Wark**   Formerly capital of Tynedale's barony, and part of the huge estates of the earls of Derwentwater. After the 1715 rebellion these passed into the control of the Commissioners of Greenwich Hospital, at whose expense in 1814–18 the newly-created parish churches of Wark, Greystead, and Humshaugh were built, all to a similar neat design, by Seward, Sir John Soane's pupil. Wark village has two-storey, grey stone cottages round a small green dominated by a fine chestnut. An imposing Mechanics Institute is a reminder of mid-Victorian enthusiasm for adult education, while in the churchyard Abel Chapman's grave commemorates one of the greatest sportsman-naturalists.

**West Woodburn**   Semi-industrial village in Redesdale where A68 swoops down hill to cross river. Dere Street is just to the west. Ruined peles in vicinity are evidence of vulnerability during Border troubles. On brow of hill to north a re-erected Roman milestone stands by a gateway. Roadside spoil-heaps on hills south-east are evidence of former ironstone working. At Ridsdale, a castle-like structure west of the road is ruined engine-house that powered the Ridsdale ironworks around middle of last century.

**Whittingham**   Agreeable, picturesque village on River Aln a few miles east of National Park boundary, at centre of Whittingham Vale. Heavily-restored church has Saxon quoins in west tower; fourteenth-century pele-tower converted into almshouse 1845 but now empty. River bisects village, footbridge links linear groups of stone cottages on north with green, trees, and more neat cottages on south. Castle Inn, near bridge, was posting house for Newcastle–Edinburgh coaches which came this way before road diverted eastwards. Whittingham Fair remembered now only in song (same tune as 'Scarborough Fair').

**\*Williemoteswick**   At the end of a minor road beyond Beltingham, south of the Tyne opposite Bardon Mill. Fortified manor-house of the Ridleys, now a working farm, with entrance to courtyard beneath fourteenth-century gatehouse. Worth walking up farm track to south to savour wider view of Tyne valley, and appreciate large group of farm buildings.

**\*Windy Gyle**   Appropriately named rounded summit on Cheviot ridge, at 2,030ft (619m). Russell's Carn, a Bronze Age monument, named after Lord Francis Russell, killed nearby in 1585 at a meeting of Wardens of the Marches. Pennine Way strides along the Border here, and nearest road, in Coquet valley, is 3 miles (4.8km) to the south.

**Winshields**   At 1,132ft (345m) the highest point along the Roman Wall. It looks and feels it, with stunning panoramas rewarding the easy, short climb from

Steel Rigg car-park. On its crest, Turret T40A would have been the windiest of signalling and lookout posts.

**Wooler**   Small town by Wooler Water, where Cheviots descend to Milfield Plain. Hill and arable farming meet, meriting grant of market about 1200, although livestock market importance dates only from seventeenth century. Close-clustered stone houses, grey-pink and rather dour, grouped round small triangular Market Place at southern end of High Street. Hotels and inns compete for attention: Red Lion, 1671, has two-storeyed, gothicised porch, while Black Bull opposite, 1910, has two-storeyed bow windows separated apparently by boiler-plates. Angel is next door, with Wheatsheaf at top of Peth Head, where colour-washed cottages make pleasant group balancing terrace above Market Place. Cheviot Street, with Anchor Inn at corner, leads past traditional Northumbrian cottages to Middleton, and was old way from south into town.

High Street, largely rebuilt after disastrous 1863 fire, has some late-Victorian shop-fronts, a Mechanics Institute, 1889, with houses nearby showing a distinct inward lean. Church Street descends from Market Place; St Mary's is externally Victorian, internally 1765, and adjoins mound where Wooler tower once stood. Shop opposite, steeply-gabled with pantiles replacing earlier thatched roof. Nearby Tenter Hill is a neat row of single-storey white-washed cottages above a sloping green, the name recalling associations with eighteenth-century wool processing.

Routing of Newcastle–Edinburgh road through town in 1830 brought increased traffic and importance, and Tankerville Arms, at northern end, was important post house and coaching inn. A697 now bypasses it, but sensible travellers find Wooler's friendly welcome justifies the small detour. Car parking no problem. Good centre for exploring area of northern Cheviots. (Market day Wednesday).

**\*Yeavering Bell**   Steep-sided on its northern flanks, this smooth, grassy hill has on its summit the most impressive and extensive Iron Age settlement in the area. A stone rampart encloses an area of 13 acres (5.5ha) with the identified remains of 130 hut-circles, representing, for its time, an unusually large community. We probably appreciate the expansive northward view more that they did.

# BIBLIOGRAPHY

Allsop, B. and Clark, U. *Historic Architecture of Northumberland* (Oriel Press, 1969)

Bailey, J. and Culley, G. *General View of the Agriculture of the County of Northumberland, 1794*

Bonser, K. J. *The Drovers* (Macmillan, 1970)

Collier, C. and Stewart, L. A. *Wooler and Glendale: A Brief History* (Wooler, 1986)

Davies, H. *A Walk Along the Wall* (Weidenfeld and Nicolson, 1974)

Davis, C. D. Ward *The Great Parish of Simonburn* (Frank Graham, 1985)

Defoe, D. *A Tour Through Great Britain 1724–6*

Dixon, D. D. *Upper Coquetdale, Northumberland, 1904* (Reprint by Sandhill Press, Alnwick, 1987) (A classic of local history)

Dixon, H. *An Allendale Miscellany* (Frank Graham, 1974)

Forestry Commission *The Kielder Forests, 1982*

Graham, Frank *Rothbury and Coquetdale* (Frank Graham, 1975)
*The Castles of Northumberland* (Frank Graham, 1976)
*Tynedale from Blanchland to Carter Bar* (Frank Graham, 1978)

Hopkins, Tony *Northumberland National Park* (Countryside Commission Official Guide. Webb & Bower, 1987) (A clear, concise, well-illustrated introduction to the Northumberland National Park)

Hunt, C. J. *The Lead Miners of the Northern Pennines* (Manchester University Press, 1970)

MacCord, N. *An Introduction to the History of Upper North Tynedale* (Newcastle, 1982)

Manley, G. *Climate and the British Scene* (Collins, 1952)

Margary, I. D. *Roman Roads in Britain* (Baker, 1973)

Newton, R. *The Northumberland Landscape* (Hodder & Stoughton, 1972)

Northumberland National Park, and Countryside Dept *A Field Guide to the Cheviot Hills* (1985)
*A Field Guide to the Hadrian's Wall Area* (1986) (Although these are aimed at school and college groups, they are so well written and illustrated to be of great interest to visitors in general)

*Walks in the Cheviot Hills* (1986)

*Walks in Coquetdale* (1986)

*Walks in the Hadrian's Wall Area* (1985)

(Models of what good walks guides should be, combining clear writing, local history and natural history, with excellent illustrations and 1:25,000 map sections)

*The Story of Redesdale* (1986) (Concise, readable, well-illustrated local history)

Northumberland Wildlife Trust *Nature Reserves of the Northumberland Wildlife Trust* (Newcastle, 1975)

Pawson, H. C. *The Agricultural Survey of Northumberland 1961*

Pearsall, W. H. *Mountains and Moorland* (Collins, 1958)

Pevsner, N. and Richmond, I. *Northumberland* (Penguin, 1957)

Raistrick, A. *The Pennine Dales* (Eyre & Spottiswode, 1968)

Ramblers' Association *Ramblers' Tynedale* (1975)

  *Rambles Through Northumberland* (Harold Hill, 1977)

Robson, D. A. *A Guide to the Geology of the Cheviot Hills* (Trans. National History Society of Northumberland and Durham, Vol 43. No1. 1976)

  *A Guide to the Geology of Northumberland and The Border* (Trans. Natural History Society of Northumberland and Durham, 1965)

Rowland, T. H. *The Alemouth or Corn Road* (Alnwick, 1982)

  *Dere Street* (Frank Graham, 1974)

Stamp, L. D. *Britain's Structure and Scenery* (Collins, 1946, 1975)

Stephenson, T. *The Pennine Way* (HMSO, 1969)

Trevelyan, G. M. *The Middle Marches* (Frank Graham, 1976) (Reprint of the great historian's classic essay first published separately in 1926.)

Trueman, A. E. *Geology and Scenery in England and Wales* (Penguin, 1949, 1971)

Wainwright, A. *Pennine Way Companion* (Westmorland Gazette, 1968)

Warn, C. R. *Rural Branch Lines of Northumberland (Frank Graham, 1978)*

Watson, G. *Northumberland Villages* (Robert Hale, 1976)

White, J. T. *The Scottish Border and Northumberland* (Eyre Methuen, 1973)

Wilson, R. J. A. *A Guide to the Roman Remains in Britain* (Constable, 1975)

In addition to the above, an increasing number of useful booklets and leaflets are produced by the Northumberland National Park and Countryside Department, the Northumbrian Water Authority, The National Trust, the Forestry Commission and English Heritage about places, activities, and specialised interests.

# INDEX

Page numbers in **bold** indicate illustrations